# Utilizing Prior Research in Evaluation Planning

David S. Cordray, *Editor*

**NEW DIRECTIONS FOR PROGRAM EVALUATION**
**A Publication of the Evaluation Research Society**
ERNEST R. HOUSE, MARK W. LIPSEY, *Editors-in-Chief*

Number 27, September 1985

Paperback sourcebooks in
The Jossey-Bass Higher Education and
Social and Behavioral Sciences Series

Jossey-Bass Inc., Publishers
San Francisco • London

David S. Cordray (Ed.).
*Utilizing Prior Research in Evaluation Planning.*
New Directions for Program Evaluation, no. 27.
San Francisco: Jossey-Bass, 1985.

**New Directions for Program Evaluation Series**
A Publication of the Evaluation Research Society
Ernest R. House, Mark W. Lipsey, *Editors-in-Chief*

Copyright © 1985 by Jossey-Bass Inc., Publishers
and
Jossey-Bass Limited

Copyright under International, Pan American, and Universal Copyright Conventions. All rights reserved. No part of this issue may be reproduced in any form—except for brief quotation (not to exceed 500 words) in a review or professional work—without permission in writing from the publishers.

*New Directions for Program Evaluation* (publication number USPS 449-050) is published quarterly by Jossey-Bass Inc., Publishers, and is sponsored by the Evaluation Research Society. Second-class postage rates are paid at San Francisco, California, and at additional mailing offices.

*Correspondence:*
Subscriptions, single-issue orders, change of address notices, undelivered copies, and other correspondence should be sent to Subscriptions, Jossey-Bass Inc., Publishers, 433 California Street, San Francisco, California 94104.

Editorial correspondence should be sent to the Editors-in-Chief, Ernest House, CIRCE-270, Education Building, University of Illinois, Champaign, Ill. 61820.

Library of Congress Catalog Card Number 85-60836

International Standard Serial Number ISSN 0164-7989

International Standard Book Number ISBN 87589-765-7

Cover art by WILLI BAUM

Manufactured in the United States of America

# *Ordering Information*

The paperback sourcebooks listed below are published quarterly and can be ordered either by subscription or single-copy.

Subscriptions cost $40.00 per year for institutions, agencies, and libraries. Individuals can subscribe at the special rate of $30.00 per year *if payment is by personal check*. (Note that the full rate of $40.00 applies if payment is by institutional check, even if the subscription is designated for an individual.) Standing orders are accepted.

Single copies are available at $9.95 when payment accompanies order, and *all single-copy orders under $25.00 must include payment*. (California, New Jersey, New York, and Washington, D.C., residents please include appropriate sales tax.) For billed orders, cost per copy is $9.95 plus postage and handling. (Prices subject to change without notice.)

Bulk orders (ten or more copies) of any individual sourcebook are available at the following discounted prices: 10-49 copies, $8.95 each; 50-100 copies, $7.96 each; over 100 copies, *inquire*. Sales tax and postage and handling charges apply as for single copy orders.

To ensure correct and prompt delivery, all orders must give either the *name of an individual* or an *official purchase order number*. Please submit your order as follows:

*Subscriptions:* specify series and year subscription is to begin.
*Single Copies:* specify sourcebook code (such as, PE1) and first two words of title.

Mail orders for United States and Possessions, Latin America, Canada, Japan, Australia, and New Zealand to:
 Jossey-Bass Inc., Publishers
 433 California Street
 San Francisco, California 94104

Mail orders for all other parts of the world to:
 Jossey-Bass Limited
 28 Banner Street
 London EC1Y 8QE


*New Directions for Program Evaluation*
Ernest R. House, Mark W. Lipsey, *Editors-in-Chief*

PE1 *Exploring Purposes and Dimensions,*, Scarvia B. Anderson, Claire D. Coles
PE2 *Evaluating Federally Sponsored Programs*, Charlotte C. Rentz, R. Robert Rentz
PE3 *Monitoring Ongoing Programs*, Donald L. Grant
PE4 *Secondary Analysis*, Robert F. Boruch

| | |
|---|---|
| PE5 | *Utilization of Evaluative Information,* Larry A. Braskamp, Robert D. Brown |
| PE6 | *Measuring the Hard-to-Measure,* Edward H. Loveland |
| PE7 | *Values, Ethics, and Standards in Evaluation,* Robert Perloff, Evelyn Perloff |
| PE8 | *Training Program Evaluators,* Lee Sechrest |
| PE9 | *Assessing and Interpreting Outcomes,* Samuel Ball |
| PE10 | *Evaluation of Complex Systems,* Ronald J. Wooldridge |
| PE11 | *Measuring Effectiveness,* Dan Baugher |
| PE12 | *Federal Efforts to Develop New Evaluation Methods,* Nick L. Smith |
| PE13 | *Field Assessments of Innovative Evaluation Methods,* Nick L. Smith |
| PE14 | *Making Evaluation Research Useful to Congress,* Leonard Saxe, Daniel Koretz |
| PE15 | *Standards for Evaluation Practice,* Peter H. Rossi |
| PE16 | *Applications of Time Series Analysis to Evaluation,* Garlie A. Forehand |
| PE17 | *Stakeholder-Based Evaluation,* Anthony S. Bryk |
| PE20 | *Developing Effective Internal Evaluation,* Arnold J. Love |
| PE21 | *Making Effective Use of Mailed Questionnaires,* David J. Bowering |
| PE22 | *Secondary Analysis of Available Data Bases,* David J. Bowering |
| PE23 | *Evaluating the New Information Technologies,* Jerome Johnston |
| PE24 | *Issues in Data Synthesis,,* William H. Yeaton, Paul M. Wortman |
| PE25 | *Culture and Evaluation,* Michael Quinn Patton |
| PE26 | *Economic Evaluations of Public Programs,* James S. Catterall |

# *Contents*

Editor's Notes 1
David S. Cordray

Chapter 1. Evaluation: The State of the Art and the Sorry State of the Science 7
*Mark W. Lipsey, Scott Crosse, Jan Dunkle, John Pollard, Gordon Stobart*
A review of the methodological underpinnings of prior evaluations reveals serious conceptual and analytical flaws. Vigorous, causal, theoretically thoughtful, and methodologically sound experimental research should be conducted when conditions permit. When these conditions are not met, alternative approaches should be chosen.

Chapter 2. Quantitative Synthesis: An Actuarial Base for Planning Impact Evaluations 29
*David S. Cordray, L. Joseph Sonnefeld*
Relying on selected prior studies to plan impact evaluations may be risky. Accumulating evidence across multiple assessments provides a basis for judging the likelihood of design flaws and aids both micro-level and macro-level planning.

Chapter 3. Using Measures of Treatment Strength and Integrity in Planning Research 49
*William H. Yeaton*
The strength and integrity of the treatment are central to the planning and interpretation of evaluation studies. When they are not explicitly assessed or reported in prior research, estimates of their magnitudes can be inferred from the nature and scope of the intervention.

Chapter 4. Using Program Information to Plan Evaluations 63
*Sherry Holland*
The political, situational, and contextual aspects of a treatment environment place constraints on the evaluation design. Client characteristics must also be considered. For some national programs, data exist that can facilitate planning decisions.

Chapter 5. Obstacles to Using Prior Research and Evaluations 79
*Robert G. Orwin*
Deficient reporting by primary researchers hinders the use of prior studies in planning new evaluations. Some techniques of research synthesis are proposed to partially compensate for these problems and illustrate the role and limitations of human judgement in using prior research.

*Chapter 6. Quality Control in Evaluation* 93
*William M. K. Trochim, Ronald J. Visco*
Data errors in program information that contribute to bias and noise can be detected using auditing techniques. Future studies will be higher in technical quality and more useful if systematic quality control procedures are adopted.

*Index* 107

# Editor's Notes

The professional literature on program evaluation assumes and encourages the use of prior research and evaluations in planning new studies. If we take the view that knowledge accumulates over successive assessments, previous evaluation studies should illuminate the issues to be addressed and point to successful methodological tactics. On the other hand, the pervasiveness of methodological shortcomings in the literature suggests that insufficient attention has been given to the experiences gained from prior evaluation efforts. The purpose of this volume is to delineate some of the strengths and limitations of using prior research and evaluations as a means of planning new evaluations.

Program evaluation encompasses a broad range of activities and methodologies and a short volume can be accused of doing injustice to the complex decisions associated with planning different types of evaluations. To limit the domain, the chapters focus primarily on planning impact evaluations—that is, those evaluations that are suitable for numerically estimating the effects of interventions, programs, and projects. While this emphasis may seem unnecessarily narrow to some individuals, two points can be raised in its defense. First, as Lipsey, Crosse, Dunkle, Pollard, and Stobart note (Chapter One), the experimental paradigm is the dominant approach in the published literature, albeit that many of these evaluations are poor representations of the "true" paradigm. As a second justification, the issues raised by contributors to this volume reiterate the importance of considering many types of evidence (for example, strength and integrity of treatment conditions) in devising an evaluation plan. In other words, the contributors explicitly recognize the need to broaden the planning issues to consider the context, inputs, processes, and mediational mechanisms as well as outcomes in designing impact evaluations. Prior research and evaluation can serve as a basis for determining how much is known about these dimensions. If we discover that the literature is silent on, for example, how to measure these components, and no other useful evidence can inform our decisions, we may have grounds to consider postponing an impact assessment until these more basic questions have been addressed.

A discussion of the role of prior research and evaluation would be incomplete without careful scrutiny of the quality of the knowledge base constructed from prior evaluations. An examination of other obstacles that are likely to be encountered also seems necessary. The first two chapters of this volume address these issues.

Chapter One of this volume, by Lipsey, Crosse, Dunkle, Pollard, and Stobart, serves to illustrate both the nature of current practice in evaluation and the state of the available knowledge base. Their methodological review of a sample of published evaluations shows that there is substantial room for improvement in the quality of evaluation practices and provides a general overview of prior sins of omission appearing in the published literature (for example, insufficient attention to measurement, statistical power, and program theory). Since their assessment encompasses a broad spectrum of substantive areas (for example, mental health and criminal justice), the problems they identify occur in a wide range of areas.

Chapter One questions the utility of prior research and evaluation as a means of planning new impact evaluations. These concerns are not new, of course. Quantitative syntheses (Glass, McGaw, and Smith, 1981; Light and Pillemer, 1984) and secondary analyses (Boruch, Wortman, and Cordray, 1981; Wolins, 1982) have demonstrated that some types of evaluation methods produce untrustworthy results, making their utility for planning questionable. Further, competition for journal space, vague or nonexistent guidelines for reporting procedures and results, and uncertainties inherent in translating evaluation practices into written accounts further degrade the usefulness of prior research and evaluations. Given these problems, how can prior evaluations help facilitate the planning process?

The answer is relatively simple. We examine the methodological underpinnings of both the poor and exemplary studies to guide us: prior mistakes illustrate the pitfalls to be avoided and creative solutions are provided by the exemplary studies. Most attention to date has focused on methods for increasing the chances of implementing high quality research designs. However, more recent discussions take a broader view of the planning process and emphasize joint consideration of sampling, design, measurement of context, inputs, process, outcomes, and statistical analysis. These more realistic models of the assessment process (see, Chen and Rossi, 1983) require more planning and thus more consideration of prior research and evaluation.

Evaluation plans often meet with considerable resistance when they are implemented. Currently, it is agreed that programs and program environments may not conform to the planner's expectations. It is unreasonable to assume that the program will be implemented according to the written and oral testimony of its developers, and provisions must be made to understand departures from the original program. As Lipsey and others (Chapter One) discuss, if a program does not produce its intended effects, questions are raised as to whether the theory underlying the intervention was in error, the integrity of service delivery was threatened, or the treatment package was too weak to produce the intended effects. Since these are recent concerns, it is unlikely that prior research and evaluations will be informative. Yeaton (Chapter Three), while echoing the concern raised by Lipsey and others, enumerates ways to gauge the strength and integrity of treatments even if the authors do not explicitly measure these components or report the results.

Further, program developers may overestimate the demand for their program. When fewer individuals enroll than expected, the implications are usually obvious. A successful intervention may go unnoticed due to insufficient statistical power induced by a smaller than expected number of participants. In Chapter Two, Cordray and Sonnefeld illustrate some of the micro-level planning decisions (for example, choosing a sample size, specifying the magnitude of the effect, and determining the duration of the trial and the timing of postintervention assessment) that must be made in specifying the operational details of a clinical trial to assess the impact of a psycho-educational intervention. Quantitative synthesis methodology is proposed as a way to augment the basis for these decisions. By systematically extracting and recording information about the methodological underpinnings for a collection of relevant studies, the planner can, as a by-product of meta-analysis, develop an actuarial base for making planning decisions. The application of this strategy is illustrated by using evidence obtained from two recent meta-analyses.

In most meta-analyses, the information on methodological characteristics about primary evaluations is woefully incomplete. To a certain extent, this limits their utility. Reporting deficiencies discussed by Orwin (Chapter Five) and the neglect of important issues (for example, measurement sensitivity) further reduce the utility of these primary evaluations for planning new evaluations. Corrective actions would entail more deliberate consideration by meta-analyst's of what to extract from prior research and evaluations. For the primary evaluator, improved data collection and reporting in future studies would also contribute to long term utility. For now, the tactics suggested by Yeaton (Chapter Three) and Orwin (Chapter Five) can partially overcome these problems.

Holland (Chapter Four) takes a position similar to that offered by Cordray and Sonnefeld. The main difference is that she focuses on the use of a national data base as a way to examine the context and environment within which drug rehabilitation programs are implemented. To characterize the type of planning information that would be helpful, Holland suggests a model of factors that impinge on treatment. In addition to identifying how this data can be used, the contents of the national data base are assessed against the model. While useful for gaining a general understanding of the constraints imposed by situational factors, a number of shortcomings limit the utility of these forms of program information.

Other obstacles to using prior research are discussed in Chapter Five by Orwin, with an emphasis on systematic research synthesis. He describes how the manner in which information is reported in primary studies can influence their utility. Deficient reporting in evaluation studies, for example, is a pervasive deterrent to using prior evidence. Rather than ignoring studies that are poorly or incompletely reported, Orwin identifies a set of partial solutions that could be employed until reporting is improved. These methods provide a way of using available evidence but require that we systematically account for its differential utility. Orwin's second theme concerns the role of human judgment in extracting information from prior research and evaluations. His argument is that some information is more difficult to categorize, rate, or summarize and, as such, is more prone to error. Using prior research to plan subsequent studies depends on the availability of evidence and the planner's capacity to accurately extract it. Some solutions are suggested to ameliorate these difficulties.

Finally, Trochim and Visco (Chapter Six) argue that the auditing profession could serve as a useful role model for incorporating a quality control mechanism in the evaluation. They illustrate key auditing principles that could strengthen the sensitivity of future assessments by reducing the extraneous sources of "noise" introduced by field conditions. While their focus is prospective, they are particularly concerned about the quality of the evidence produced in school districts because of prior research on errors in this data.

In planning this volume, the intent was to provide some concrete guidance on using prior research and evaluation to plan new evaluation studies. The contributors have tried to balance optimism with reality. For one thing, the idea of relying on a pre-and post-test experimental design now appears to be unrealistic. Also, the shift in impact assessments is away from the issue of establishing whether a program produced its intended effects and toward more comprehensive assessments that examine why a program produced positive, null, or negative effects. These questions considered by the authors have been stimulated by an interest in accumulating evidence (meta-analysis) as well as the sobering experience of having to answer to program managers, decision makers, and colleagues about why interventions do not seem to ameliorate the problems they are intended to solve. This level of inquiry expands the planning process tremendously and places a substantial burden on the planner. Some of that burden may be lifted through careful examination of the efforts of prior studies.

Another important point is that planning is uncertain. If we are accurate in our assessment of the complexity of the evaluation tasks, the study may yield timely, high quality, and useful results. However, unpredictable changes in circumstances can undermine even the most thoughtful and well justified plan. The main point in planning is to match the total methodological strategy with the realities of the setting within which a program, project, or intervention will be examined. As implementation of the plan begins, trade-offs among the elements of the methodological system are inevitable. A principal question for the planner is how to gauge the importance of various compromises. Prior research should continue to serve as a guide to resolve issues as they emerge throughout the evaluation.

Rather than being the blind man attempting to determine which end of the elephant we are assessing, perhaps it's time to "cheat" a bit by peeking under the blindfold.

David S. Cordray<br>
Editor

## References

Boruch, R. F., Wortman, P. M., and Cordray, D. S., and Associates (Eds.). *Reanalyzing Program Evaluations: Policies and Practices for Secondary Analysis of Social and Educational Programs.* San Francisco: Jossey-Bass, 1981

Chen, H-T., and Rossi, P. H. "Evaluating with Sense: The Theory Driven Approach." *Evaluation Review,* 1983 7, 283–302.

Glass, G. V., McGaw, B., and Smith, M. L. *Meta-Analysis in Social Research.* Beverly Hills, Calif.: Sage, 1981.

Light, R. J., and Pillemer, D. B. *Summing Up: The Science of Reviewing Research.* Cambridge, Mass. Harvard University Press, 1984.

Wolins, L. *Research Mistakes in Social and Behavioral Sciences.* Ames: Iowa State University Press, 1982.

*David S. Cordray is group director for public assistance and federal evaluation policy in the Program Evaluation and Methodology Division at the U.S. General Accounting Office, Washington, D.C., and associate professor of psychology at Northwestern University. (The statements and opinions expressed in this volume do not represent official U.S. General Accounting Office policy.)*

*A representative sample of studies drawn from the published program evaluation literature is systematically examined. Weak designs, low statistical power, ad hoc measurement, and neglect of treatment implementation and program theory characterize the state of the art in program evaluation. Program evaluation research under the experimental paradigm requires better planning and execution.*

# Evaluation: The State of the Art and the Sorry State of the Science

*Mark W. Lipsey, Scott Crosse, Jan Dunkle, John Pollard, Gordon Stobart*

The dominant methodological approach to program evaluation research today is based on the experimental paradigm, that is quantitative measurement of dependent variables with controlled designs to establish cause-and-effect relationships. Though the universal appropriateness of this paradigm for program evaluation has been vigorously disputed in some quarters, most of the studies actually conducted and publicly disseminated under the program evaluation label nonetheless embody at least the rudiments of experimental design. The telltale signs of quantitative measurement, some attempt at control or baseline groups, and cause-and-effect thinking are present even when there is otherwise little resemblance to the classical randomized experiment.

It is also widely acknowledged that program evaluation is often poorly done within the experimental paradigm. It has been commonplace for reviews of selected program evaluation research to sharply criticize the methodology of the studies examined. For example, Bernstein and Freeman (1975) reviewed 236 federally sponsored evaluation studies and concluded that at least half the studies that evaluated impact were "deficient either in design, sampling, or validity of measures" (p. 97). A similar conclusion was reached by Gordon and Morse (1975) after close examination of a sample of 93 program evaluation studies published in sociological journals.

The difficulty of doing good experimental work under program evaluation circumstances can be attributed to at least two rather different factors. First, as has often been noted, there are numerous practical difficulties inherent in the matching of good research design to practical program circumstances. Weiss (1972) described the program context as "intrinsically inhospitable" to the methods of social science. Secondly, social scientists for the most part are not very well trained to do methodologically exacting research under field conditions. Applied research has been a neglected stepchild in many of the social science disciplines that confer higher prestige on theoretical work and basic research. Ironically, the more that evaluation researchers learn about appropriate application of experimental methodology in program evaluation settings, the more difficult the research becomes. Thoughtful evaluation researchers struggling to understand the complex phenomena of social programs with the available tools have increasingly differentiated the range of substantive and methodological concerns with which, to be cogent, the research must deal.

*Key Aspects of Program Evaluation Research.* Our purpose here is to review and assess current practice in program evaluation research under the experimental paradigm with special attention to some relatively neglected issues that have only recently become prominent in the literature. In order to provide a framework for this task, we have attempted to extract the most important methodological and conceptual imperatives from the metaliterature in program evaluation research, that is, the literature discussing how program evaluation should be done. The result is five factors that, once articulated, take on the character of common sense. Their essential role in program evaluation is readily apparent and neglect of them makes program evaluation under the experimental paradigm difficult to interpret.

*Research Design.* Only reaffirmation is required on this topic since design issues are the oldest and most thoroughly discussed of the methodological concerns that face evaluation researchers. At issue, of course, is valid identification of the cause-and-effect linkages central to the experimental paradigm. Proper research design is required to determine if a particular effect is actually produced by a particular intervention and to separate the effect of the intervention from other happenstances that have similar effects. A valid determination of causal links requires that the research design include proper controls. Campbell has been the most influential advocate for the use of randomized control groups in such research and has systematized the concept of quasi-experiments as approximations to controlled experiments (Campbell and Stanley, 1966; Cook and Campbell, 1979). From the present perspective, the striking thing about this topic is the great volume of literature and methodological advice available and the general awareness of the pertinent issues among evaluation researchers. By comparison, other important methodological issues have been sorely neglected.

*Statistical Power.* Statistical power is the probability of a statistically significant result on a dependent measure when there is, in fact, a real effect produced by the treatment. Power is an important matter in program evaluation research for at least two reasons. First, there is good reason to believe that statistical power is often quite low for research done under field conditions. Boruch and Gomez (1979) have shown that the inconsistent treatment delivery and increased measurement error likely in the field degrade statistical power by multiplicative factors. Moreover, such research is often done under practical constraints that limit the available sample size, which in itself limits power. Second, statistical power is important in program evaluation because of its close relationship to Type II error, the probability of accepting the null hypothesis of no treatment effect when, in fact, it is false. While Type I error receives predominant concern in theoretical research, it can be argued that Type II error is of equal or greater importance in practical research. Such error means that the research finds no effect for a program or treatment that is genuinely effective. In the political context of program evaluation research, a null result will almost certainly be interpreted as program failure and may produce practical difficulties for the program, that is, diminished support from sponsors or funders, staff demoralization, reputational injury, and so forth. Research with low statistical power thus has the potential for falsely branding a program as a failure when, in fact, the problem is the inability of the research to detect an effect, not the inability of the program to produce one.

*Measurement.* It is fundamental that, without outcome measures that are sensitive to potential program effects, adequate assessment of those effects cannot be made. Measurement sensitivity is a somewhat unfamiliar term for applied researchers (see Aiken, 1977), but it has the advantage of encompassing the traditional issues of reliability and validity while emphasizing the ultimate responsiveness of the measures to the effects of interest. Dependent measures can fail to respond to underlying treatment effects because they: (1) lack validity (do not measure the construct on which change occurs), (2) lack reliability (contain so much measurement error that change variance is obscured), or (3) lack sensitivity (do not respond proportionately to changes on the construct of interest) (see Carver, 1974). Lipsey (1983) demonstrated the interplay of validity, reliability, and sensitivity in the measurement of surrogate treatment effects deliberately constructed to simulate large differences. The results indicated that inadequate measurement easily obscures important treatment effects under program evaluation circumstances. Measurement issues are thus closely related to statistical power since they influence the apparent effect size that in turn, is one of the major determinants of statistical power (Sechrest and Yeaton, 1981; 1982).

*Treatment Implementation.* It is a truism that a treatment that is not actually implemented and delivered cannot have effects. Moreover, even if implemented, a trivial or inappropriate treatment relative to the problem it addresses will not have effects either. Sechrest and his collaborators (Sechrest and Redner, 1979; Sechrest and others 1979; Yeaton and Sechrest, 1981) have taken the lead in specifying the treatment characteristics necessary to reasonably expect an effect. In their language, a treatment must have adequate strength and integrity. That is, it must, in principle, be sufficiently powerful to alter the condition being treated and it must be fully delivered according to the intended regimen. Methodologically, some independent check is required on the integrity of the treatment implementation as well as a conceptual framework that plausibly links the nature and level of the treatment to the expected effects as measured. Dilution of the treatment as implemented, through low dosage, weak or inconsistent delivery, and so forth, causes a sharp drop in the effects that can be expected and, consequently, in the likelihood that an evaluation study will detect positive effects (Boruch and Gomez, 1979).

*Program Theory.* It is becoming increasingly apparent that adequate program evaluation cannot be done by representing treatments as black box processes, either present or absent in a specific case but otherwise working through unspecified mechanisms. An insight of the evaluability assessment concept (Rutman, 1980; Wholey, 1977) is the recognition that a program is as much a conceptual construction as an organizational one. In its essence, a program consists of a set of rational linkages between program activities and expected outcomes abstracted from the particular behaviors in which program personnel happen to engage. If there is not at least an implicit program model in the conceptual sense, there is virtually no program to evaluate and no basis for determining what effects it could be expected to have or the circumstances to which it might generalize. Chen and Rossi (1981, 1983) describe the virtues of designing program evaluation around specifiable program theory. Among those virtues are: (1) the methodological advantages of identifying likely program effects that may not be stated in program goals, (that is, being able to look in the right place for effects), (2) defining intermediate or intervening effects that may signal at least partial success in advance of a longer term outcome, and (3) anticipating and managing obfuscatory variance from interactions of participant characteristics with treatment processes.

**Sources of Null Results.** Another way to state the various key aspects of program evaluation research is to analyze the sources of potential null results, that is evaluation results that show no program effects and thus, at least provisionally, conclude that the programs being evaluated failed to produce the intended effects (see Weiss, 1972). Null results can be produced by:

1. *Methods failure.* The research design may not be adequate to properly isolate the effects produced by the treatment. Statistical power may be inadequate. Outcome measures may be insensitive to treatment effects or the wrong measures may be taken. These and related problems represent a failure of the research, not necessarily a failure of the program being evaluated. They must be ruled out before any further statements can be made with confidence about the impact of the program itself.

2. *Implementation failure.* The treatment may not be delivered in sufficient dosage or coverage to have an effect. This might result through failure to deliver the full treatment as intended to all targeted recipients or through application of a potentially effective treatment in a dosage too weak to have results. Problems such as these represent program failure, but at a largely operational level that may have little bearing on the validity of the program concept itself.

3. *Theory failure.* The program concept may be wrong or misleading. Program activities may not, in fact, produce the effects expected even when they are implemented as intended. Program concepts may fail miserably and be discarded as part of trial and error learning about social intervention, or they may fail partially and be the basis for modification or reform that produces more promising approaches.

## Current Practice: Some Descriptive Data

Forceful articulation of the essential features of adequate program evaluation under the experimental paradigm has occurred relatively recently. Moreover, it has only been since about the mid-1970s that program evaluation research has emerged as a distinct specialty field with its own training programs, textbooks, professional organizations, and codified standards for evaluation research practice. This increased disciplinary integrity and self-awareness should result in a steadily improving quality of work. It is illuminating, therefore, to assess recent program evaluation practice within the experimental paradigm against the five key research considerations described above.

The authors of this chapter and those who assisted them (known collectively as the Program Evaluation Research Group) have been engaged in an ongoing project to identify, sample, and describe published evaluation studies of recent vintage. Data from that project can be used to characterize current practice with regard to research design, statistical power, measurement sensitivity, treatment implementation, and program theory. We will first describe the general nature of that project and then review the pertinent findings.

*Methods and Procedures.* Using a broad and thorough search strategy, program evaluation studies listed in the 1978–1980 volumes of *Psychological Abstracts, Sociological Abstracts,* and *The Current Index to Journals in Education* were first identified and compiled into a master bibliography. A study was identified as program evaluation if it met two criteria: (1) that there be a distinct program or policy designed and implemented to accomplish some social purpose, and (2) that the study present a more or less systematic assessment of at least some of the accomplishments of that program. In other words, there had to be a program and there had to be some sort of evaluation of it.

The bibliography of 617 items that resulted was stratified by general program area (for example, mental health, education) and a random sample of 205 references was drawn proportionately across the strata. A sustained attempt was then made to locate and photocopy each sampled article. To date, 198 of the sampled articles have been obtained, 97 percent of the total. Of those, 30 were judged not to meet the criteria for program evaluation research when the full report was examined and these were eliminated from the sample.

Each of the remaining 168 reports was then read by one of the members of the Program Evaluation Research Group, all of whom were familiar with program evaluation research, and the characteristics of the research were coded onto a form that assessed program context, treatment implementation, measurement, design, program outcome, author conclusions, overall quality, and related matters (a total of 148 variables). This coding form had been developed after examining the schemes used by other researchers (Gordon and Morse, 1975) and thoroughly discussing the issues among the members of the Program Evaluation Research Group. It was pilot tested on a sample of ten of the articles and minor adjustments in wording and format were made. An assessment of the reliability of the coding was made by having a second coder recode 18 of the reports drawn randomly. The mean agreement between coders over the 148 variables and the 18 articles at that point was 85 percent. The coding categories producing the largest coder disagreements were subsequently reviewed, redefined after discussion, and all studies were recoded on those items using the clarified definitions. Seven of the 168 articles coded reported two different evaluation research studies, each of which was coded separately, making a total of 175 studies in the analysis.

*Results.* We note first the dominance of the experimental paradigm and its variations in the methodological approach taken by the studies in our sample (see Table 1). Recall that our definition of what constituted program evaluation research was liberal, with no specification of appropriate methodology. Indeed, we particularly wanted to represent qualitative and unconventional approaches. Despite that inclusive sampling, more than two-thirds of the research designs were of a quantitative-comparative sort,

Table 1. Methodological Approach Taken in the Total Sample of Studies

|  | Number of Studies | Proportion of Total |
|---|---|---|
| *Quantitative-Comparative* | | |
| Randomized experiments | 33 | |
| Quasi-experiments | 69 | |
| Prepost comparisons | 20 | |
| Subtotal | 122 | .70 |
| *Other* | | |
| Comparison against goals/history | 18 | |
| No performance baseline | 17 | |
| Qualitative | 18 | |
| Subtotal | 53 | .30 |
| TOTAL | 175 | |

modeled more or less on one of the now notorious Campbell and Stanley (1966) designs. The remaining studies were characterized by relative neglect of the internal validity issues that so concerned Campbell and Stanley. Many of them were qualitative outright or, if they presented quantitative information, made no attempt to construct a comparison baseline or judge cause-and-effect issues, that is, compared quantitative information against administratively set goals or previous program performance.

Whether the author was affiliated with an academic institution had no relationship with the type of design utilized nor did program area (for example, mental health, education). However, the relationship of the evaluator to the program was significantly associated with the type of design (Chi-square (9, $N = 175$) = 25.30, $p < .01$). The pattern of relationships indicated that when the evaluator had been the designer of the program, the evaluation was much more likely to utilize a stronger experimental design. Also, the type of design was related to the timing with which the evaluation was instigated (Chi-square (12, $N = 175$) = 35.49, $p < .01$). Those evaluations begun after the program had been established for any length of time were more likely to be weaker quasi-experimental designs.

What follows is a close examination of the characteristics of the subset of 122 studies that approached the program evaluation research task with quantitative-comparative methodology, that is, the experimental paradigm. We will look in turn at each of the five components—research design, statistical power, measurement sensitivity, treatment implementation, and program theory—espoused above as essential aspects of adequate evaluation research under that paradigm.

*Research design.* Most of the research designs employed in the sample of program evaluation studies conducted under the experimental paradigm

Table 2. Characteristics of the Research Design for Studies Using the Experimental Paradigm (N=122)

|  | Number of Studies | Proportion of Total |  |
|---|---|---|---|
| *Type of Design* |  |  |  |
| Randomized experiment | 33 | .27 |  |
| Quasi-experiment | 69 | .57 |  |
| Regression-discontinuity | 1 |  | .01 |
| Time series | 10 |  | .08 |
| Nonequivalent comparison | 58 |  | .48 |
| Prepost "nonexperiment" | 20 | .16 |  |
| *Convergent Designs* |  |  |  |
| Single design alone | 68 | .56 |  |
| Single design with supplement | 40 | .33 |  |
| Multiple design, treatment variations | 2 | .02 |  |
| Multiple design, same treatment | 11 | .09 |  |
| Other | 1 | .01 |  |

were quasi-experimental comparisons (see Table 2). Among the quasi-experimental designs, most were nonequivalent comparisons, by far the weakest and most difficult to analyze and interpret (see Reichardt, 1979). Altogether, the weaker design categories (nonequivalent and prepost comparisons) were used in almost two-thirds of the studies; the remaining one-third were randomized experiments or stronger quasi-experimental designs (regression-discontinuity or time-series). Furthermore, most of the studies relied on only a single design and comparison, possibly with some noncomparative supplementary data collection (a client satisfaction survey). Only 11 percent used multiple designs to try to demonstrate convergent results or examine treatment variations.

*Statistical Power.* Only nine of the 122 quantitative-comparative studies included any mention of the statistical power of the research design and analysis that was employed to investigate program effects. The massive silence on this issue cannot, however, be interpreted to mean that statistical power was not a relevant question. On the contrary, even under generous assumptions power appeared to be quite low for the preponderance of studies. Table 3 reports the percentile distribution of the comparison group sample size for the studies reviewed and the associated statistical power under assumptions of different effect sizes, two-group t-test comparison, and conventional .05 alpha levels. Statistical power is presented in Table 3 as beta, the probability of obtaining statistical significance given that there was a true effect of specified magnitude. The effect size categories suggested by Cohen (1977) as representing "small" (1 percent of variance), "medium" (6 percent), and "large" (14 percent) effects in social science research were used to provide a range for the potential effects under investigation.

Table 3. Distribution of Comparison Group Sample Size
and Associated Statistical Power for Studies
Using the Experimental Paradigm (Alpha = .05)

|  |  | Statistical Power for Assumed Effect Sizes (% Variance) | | |
| --- | --- | --- | --- | --- |
| Sample Size Percentile | Sample Size | "Small" 1 percent | "Medium" 6 percent | "Large" 14 percent |
| 10 | 7 | .07 | .15 | .31 |
| 20 | 11 | .07 | .20 | .43 |
| 30 | 17 | .09 | .29 | .62 |
| 40 | 27 | .11 | .43 | .82 |
| 50 | 39 | .14 | .58 | .94 |
| 60 | 59 | .19 | .76 | .99 |
| 70 | 90 | .26 | .91 | >.99 |
| 80 | 116 | .33 | .96 | >.99 |
| 90 | 209 | .53 | >.99 | |
| 100 | 3735 | >.99 | >.99 | >.99 |
| Expected proportion of significant results if there were true effects in all studies |  | .28 | .63 | .81 |

beta =.80
beta =.95

Cohen suggested beta = .80 as a reasonable level for statistical power in general social science research, that is, a .20 chance of Type II error along with the conventional .05 chance of Type I error. As noted earlier, a case can be made that Type II errors in program evaluation are much more serious than in nonapplied research and statistical power levels should accordingly be kept higher, perhaps as high as .95.

Table 3 shows that by either standard the statistical power of the evaluation studies published in recent literature fell far short. For detection of relatively small effects or, equivalently, larger effects in high noise environments, more than 90 percent of the statistical comparisons reported fell short of the desirable power level. Sixty percent of the comparisons had less than one chance in five of detecting a small effect. Even for effects of medium size, statistical power fell below the recommended .80 level for more than 60 percent of the studies. In short, most of the evaluation studies represented in this sample had very limited ability to detect program effects on the order of magnitude that social programs are most likely to produce under field conditions.

Given the demonstrably low statistical power of the comparisons made in the recent program evaluation literature, we would expect a high proportion of null results. We coded each study in our sample to indicate whether the majority of the treatment vs. control comparisons reported showed statistically significant effects or null effects. Overall, 63 percent of the studies reported a majority of statistically significant effects and the remaining 37 percent reported a majority of null effects. Curiously, these are about the proportions we would expect under the available power levels if every program did in fact have an effect of medium size. Since universal program effectiveness of that order of magnitude seems somewhat unlikely, we presume that other factors are influencing the results. Two factors capable of upwardly biasing the proportion of positive results come readily to mind. First, since the sample represented published studies, there is the possibility of publication bias—null results are less likely to be published, whether because of the reluctance of authors or of journal editors. Second, recall that a large number of the studies in this sample used quasi-experimental designs rather than randomized experiments. In many applications, quasi-experiments have been shown to exaggerate program effects in comparison to more carefully controlled experiments (Light, 1983). The evaluation studies of interest here, therefore, most likely show some unknown mix of understatement of program effects because of low statistical power and overstatement of effects because of frequent use of quasi-experimental designs and bias against publishing null results.

*Measurement.* A variety of types of dependent measures were used in the sampled evaluation studies, with psychometric tests and survey questionnaire items most frequent (see Table 4). Fewer than half of the studies used a dependent measure without alteration that had been used previously in other research; almost 40 percent of the studies used one or more measures that had been developed ad hoc for the evaluation with no reported pretesting or validation. Most striking was the general failure to report or demonstrate that the fundamental properties of the measures used were adequate for evaluation purposes. More than 70 percent of the studies made no mention of the reliability of any of the measures, 81 percent made no mention of the validity of the measures, and 93 percent made no mention of the sensitivity of the measures to the expected program effects.

On the other hand, the use of multiple dependent measures to broaden the coverage of outcome variables was quite common. Nearly all of the studies (90 percent) used more than one dependent measure and many of those had multiple follow-up measures at various stages after treatment. About one-third of the studies used multiple measures of the same outcome construct to produce some measurement triangulation on important

Table 4. Characteristics of the Dependent Measures in Studies Using the Experimental Paradigm

|  | Number of Studies | Proportion of Total |
|---|---|---|
| *Type of at Least One Measure Used* | | |
| Psychometric | 48 | .39 |
| Criterion referenced | 21 | .17 |
| Survey item | 52 | .43 |
| Judgment rating | 27 | .22 |
| Behavioral observation | 25 | .20 |
| Records or reports | 38 | .31 |
| Qualitative | 8 | .07 |
| *Source of at Least One Dependent Measure* | | |
| Developed/Used by others | 54 | .44 |
| Adapted from others | 18 | .15 |
| Developed ad hoc, pretested | 33 | .27 |
| Developed ad hoc, not pretested | 48 | .39 |
| *Measurement Properties Described or Demonstrated* | | |
| Reliability | 33 | .27 |
| Validity | 23 | .19 |
| Sensitivity | 8 | .07 |
| *Use of Multiple Measures* | | |
| Multiple dependent measures | 110 | .90 |
|    Analyzed individually | 100 | .82 |
|    Multivariate analysis | 10 | .08 |
| Construct triangulation | 41 | .34 |

*Note:* There were multiple responses allowed on the items in this table so the total in each case exceeds 122. The proportion column reports the proportion of the 122 studies with each response.

variables. Very few of the studies, however, provided a multivariate analysis of the multiple measures, making it difficult to tell the extent of their overlap or redundancy. Results were typically reported individually for each of a series of measures that were probably not truly independent.

*Treatment Implementation.* The question of interest with regard to the sample of program evaluation studies under examination here is whether the implementation of treatment was monitored and reported in sufficient detail to document its strength and integrity in each respective application. The importance of this matter is greater to the extent that the treatments were complex and administered on a variety of occasions. Under such circumstances, there is considerable opportunity for variation or dilution in

Table 5. Complexity of Treatment in Studies Using the Experimental Paradigm

|  | Number of Studies | Proportion of Total |
|---|---|---|
| Simple, administered only once | 4 | .03 |
| Simple, administered on multiple occasions | 21 | .17 |
| Complex, administered only once | 5 | .04 |
| Complex, administered on multiple occasions | 92 | .75 |

the actual treatment application from case to case. For example, if the treatment consists only of a one-time administration of a standard drug dosage, we need only know the proportion of the target group to whom the dose was given to ensure adequate treatment implementation. If the treatment is more variable and administered over multiple occasions, such as in psychotherapy, much more information is required to establish that the treatment as delivered maintained adequate strength and integrity.

Table 5 reports the categorization of the studies sampled according to the potential variability of treatment. For each program, a judgment was made with regard, first, to the complexity of the treatment, that is, how much room there was for variation from one application to another, and, second, whether it was administered on more than one occasion. Three-fourths of the studies involved treatments that were judged to be both complex and multiply administered—the very circumstance that can permit great variation in the actual amount of treatment delivered to individual recipients.

Given the possibility of great variation in the delivery of treatment in the typical program, information regarding the level and extent of treatment implementation for the sampled studies is quite pertinent. To code what type of information was reported, we dimensionalized treatment into the following five factors: (1) how many clients received it, (2) the proportion of clients who dropped out before treatment was complete, (3) the amount of treatment received (hours of contact), (4) the duration or timing of the treatment (once a week, ten week period), and, (5) the elements or components of the treatment (methadone, counseling, home visits). For each factor, we further distinguished between the reporting of facts, that is, observations and measures of what actually occurred, and the reporting of treatment format, that is, statements about the treatment plan or intent without reference to how well it was actually fulfilled. For example, a program described as weekly counseling sessions over a ten week period is reporting a treatment plan or format. But, a statement that clients received an average of 11.3 hours of counseling each over an average of 8.7 sessions reports factual information about the treatment implementation.

Table 6 presents the data regarding what was reported on each of the

Table 6. Treatment Implementation Information in Studies Using the Experimental Paradigm

| Information Reported | Number of Studies | Proportion of Total |
|---|---|---|
| Number of Clients | | |
| Facts | 89 | .75 |
| Format only | 8 | .07 |
| Neither | 22 | .19 |
| Attrition from Treatment | | |
| Facts | 43 | .36 |
| Format only | 4 | .03 |
| Neither | 72 | .61 |
| Amount/Intensity of Treatment | | |
| Facts | 32 | .27 |
| Format only | 44 | .37 |
| Neither | 43 | .36 |
| Duration/Timing of Treatment | | |
| Facts | 41 | .34 |
| Format only | 46 | .39 |
| Neither | 32 | .27 |
| Elements/Components of Treatment | | |
| Facts | 33 | .28 |
| Format only | 42 | .35 |
| Neither | 44 | .37 |

*Note:* N=119; information unavailable for three studies.

five treatment factors for those evaluation studies in the sample. The only item reported factually for a majority of the studies was the number of clients served by the program. Well less than half of the studies reported factual information regarding attrition from treatment, amount of treatment, duration or timing of treatment, or the components of treatment. Format information was provided somewhat more frequently, with the exception of attrition, but that still left sizeable proportions of the sample that reported neither format nor facts on these factors.

Another way to depict how the evaluation studies in the sample handled the possibility of variability in the delivery of treatment to the targeted recipients is to describe the nature of the independent variable that was actually entered into the design and analysis. The independent variable, of course, represents the treatment level, usually a dichotomy encoding the treatment group vs. control group contrast. Such a dichotomy, however, assumes that each member of the treatment group received the same treatment and each member of the control group received none. If variability

Table 7. Representation of the Treatment as an Independent Variable in Studies Using the Experimental Paradigm

|  | Number of Studies | Proportion of Total |
|---|---|---|
| *Categorical* | 103 | .84 |
| Group variable, one group | 24 | .20 |
| Group variable, multiple groups | 79 | .65 |
| *Differentiated* | 19 | .16 |
| Metric treatment variable | 8 | .07 |
| Multivariate representation | 11 | .09 |

in treatment delivery is expected, the independent variable can be measured in metric form, that is, varying over a continuum of values, or even represented in multivariate form combining various separately measured treatment dimensions. As Table 7 shows, the treatment variable in the sample of studies was generally defined categorically with no further differentiation of the actual amount of treatment received. Only 16 percent of the sampled studies used a more differentiated metric or multivariate representation of the treatment variable.

*Program Theory.* As Table 5 showed, almost none of the evaluations in our sample of studies investigated the relatively unvarying, one-shot type of intervention. Most of the treatments were complex and multifaceted (psychotherapy, math curriculum). Individuals receiving the treatment probably encountered a variety of experiences and uniform treatment effects would not be expected across all individuals. Furthermore, most of the treatments included in this analysis were extended in time, requiring multiple administrations to complete the program and thus introducing issues of sequencing effects, temporal variation of treatment, and potential interaction effects across the series of treatment events. From this perspective, the issue of program theory is quite relevant—most of the programs actually evaluated did not provide simple structured treatments that could be expected to work through readily apparent mechanisms.

While program theory has received increasing emphasis in the literature (Chen and Rossi, 1981, 1983), we know of no well-developed classification scheme that defines the nature and form of program theory that can be expected in evaluation studies. Our first task, therefore, was to derive inductively, from our own sample of evaluation studies, some framework for recognizing and differentiating types of program theory.

We found that four characteristics of the program description helped discriminate between different levels of theoretical sophistication. One such characteristic was the degree of explication of the intervention, that is, how well the individual program elements making up the intervention were described. The second issue was whether the program was described primarily in terms of operations and procedures, intervention strategies and philosophies, or general constructs and concepts. A third characteristic was the extent to which there was a delineation of the causal sequences relating program elements—whether the elements of intervention and outcome were related to each other in some sort of causal sequence or simply listed in more or less disconnected fashion. Finally, we found it important to note whether the program description invoked concepts specific to the particular program context or if it was placed in a larger conceptual/theoretical context.

What emerged from our application of these distinctions was a classification scheme for program theory comprised of the following categories and subcategories:

### Nontheoretical

*Black Box Treatments.* Virtually no information on the program was provided other than a descriptive label. No rationale was given as to why the intervention should work or what elements combined to form the intervention. Example: Crisis counseling was provided to all treatment participants.

### Sub-Theoretical

*Program Strategy.* Studies describing programs in this category reported a treatment strategy that was framed largely in terms of operational or service goals with little reference to the outcomes expected for clients. The program was structured around some quality of service standards and separable program components, but presented no explanation of how providing service at that standard would produce the desired impact. Example: The crisis counseling consisted of an attempt to reach the family quickly, a focus on and support of the battered spouse, and appropriate referral for followup treatment.

*Program Principles.* Studies judged to fall into this category presented general statements about the treatment and the assumed effects but no explanation of the details or the reasons why the treatment was believed to produce the expected effects. The program appeared, therefore, to be based on a belief or principle that was itself neither analyzed nor demonstrated. Example: Crisis counseling was provided to raise self-esteem and improve family communication.

### Theoretical

*Hypothesis Testing.* In this category, programs framed their efforts in terms of specific formulations linking elements of the program to desired outcomes. However, the framework was somewhat ad hoc, of limited scope, and applicable primarily to the

Table 8. Theory Types Found in Studies Using the
Experimental Paradigm

|  | Number of Studies | Proportion of Total |
|---|---|---|
| Nontheoretical | | |
| Black-box | 23 | .19 |
| Subtheoretical | 55 | .46 |
| Program strategy | 29 | .24 |
| Program principles | 26 | .22 |
| Theoretical | 35 | .29 |
| Hypothesis testing | 24 | .20 |
| Integrated theory | 11 | .09 |
| Unclassified | 6 | .05 |

Note: N=119; information unavailable for three studies.

specific program under investigation. It was represented most clearly by studies that did hypothesis testing on the particular independent and dependent variables measured in the evaluation. Example: Testing whether support to the battered spouse raised self-esteem scores, lowered willingness to tolerate physical abuse, and so on.

*Integrated Theory.* Program descriptions classified in this category provided an a priori theory within which the specific formulation of program elements, rationale, and causal linkages was embedded. The program theory was more general than the specific application represented by the program under investigation and was derived from some source other than the experience or folk wisdom of the program personnel or the evaluation researchers. Example: Social learning theory as a basis for developing techniques of assertiveness training for battered spouses.

With this classification scheme in hand, we were able to provide some review of the level of program theory reflected in our sample of evaluation studies. Table 8 presents the classification of the studies into the theory types defined above. Note, however, that the results indicate the level at which program theory was described in published evaluation studies. Whether those descriptions represented the actual level of theoretical thinking embodied in the program cannot be determined from our data.

As Table 8 indicates, approximately two-thirds of the sample of studies failed to reflect a theoretical basis any higher than what we called "Sub-theoretical." Fewer than one out of ten of the studies were judged to provide an "integrated theory" to describe the program and nearly one in five presented "black boxes." Moreover, the lack of theory development appeared to be widespread throughout the evaluation community. For example, whether the primary author of the evaluation had an academic affiliation made no difference (Chi-square (4, $N = 108$) = 4.72, $p > .30$), nor did program area (for example, mental health, education) show any relation to level of program theory (Chi-square (16, $N = 90$) = 13.94, $p > .60$).

## Conclusions

The experimental paradigm, dominant in evaluation research, is primarily concerned with investigating the causal relationships between programs viewed as social interventions and their effects on recipients. Proper assessment of such relationships requires a research design capable of isolating any true causal effects, adequate statistical power to detect real effects, measures sensitive to those effects, an actual and relatively complete implementation of the treatment so that whatever effects are possible will in fact be produced, and some information about, or at least investigation of, the mechanism by which the effects are produced.

The conclusion emerging from analysis of the present sample of evaluation studies is that evaluation research under the experimental paradigm is largely conducted at a level of marginal methodological and conceptual quality. Inferentially weak designs predominated, and the reliability, validity, and sensitivity of dependent measures were rarely demonstrated. Lack of statistical power compromised many studies, even if otherwise well designed, and precluded confident statements about program effects. Moreover, while most of the programs evaluated involved relatively complex treatments administered over multiple occasions, little information regarding the extent of treatment implementation was integrated into the analysis or even reported as background. Additionally, these complex treatments were generally described in such superficial and atheoretical form that little understanding could be gleaned of the rationale linking the chosen treatment to the expected results. The net result of these various deficiencies is a program evaluation literature with many of the trappings of scientific study and little of the substance.

One limitation of the present review is that it considered only published studies even though it is likely that the majority of program evaluation research is not formally published. We would suppose, for example, that the unpublished literature contains a lower proportion of experimental and quasi-experimental studies than found in our sample. On that basis, one might judge the experimental paradigm to be less dominant in evaluation research than we have claimed. The selection of such work for publication, however, suggests to us that it is widely viewed as the best work and thus represents a dominant image of evaluation research among practitioners even if not the most common mode. Furthermore, given disproportionate publication of evaluation studies under the experimental paradigm, we think it very unlikely that unpublished studies under that paradigm hold to higher methodological and conceptual standards than those selected by researchers, reviewers, and editors for publication. Our sample, with all its shortcomings, therefore, most probably represents higher standards than generally practiced in evaluation research.

To conclude that most evaluation research is methodologically weak only reaffirms what other reviewers have discovered about less recent work (for example, Bernstein and Freeman, 1975; Gordon and Morse, 1975). The important issue is whether methodologically deficient work in evaluation research is benign in its consequences. Collectively, evaluation research under the experimental paradigm represents our best knowledge about the effects of social programs. Does its low quality distort that knowledge or misrepresent those programs?

The effect of the methodological and conceptual problems described in this review is to render the conclusions of evaluation research highly equivocal. The widespread use of inferentially weak (nonrandomized) research designs is most likely to overestimate rather than underestimate treatment effects (for example, Light, 1983; Wortman and Yeaton, 1983), though clearly that is not always the case (see, Campbell and Erlebacher, 1970). The result of the other factors—measurement insensitivity, low statistical power, inconsistent or incomplete treatment implementation, and lack of understanding of the causal mechanism embodied in the treatment—however, is to lower the estimation of treatment effects; collectively these factors can easily render worthwhile program effects undetectable.

It is tempting to look at these two countervailing sets of factors and hope that they cancel each other out to yield program evaluation conclusions in reasonable accordance with the actual effects of the programs studied. Where judgments about individual programs are concerned, however, no such benign result is likely. Rather, a large and unknown error component is added to the results which only confounds interpretation. Statistically positive outcomes may therefore be spurious, especially if based on weak designs. Perhaps more troubling, statistically null outcomes seem likely to result all too easily from low power, insensitive measures, and weak or incomplete treatment implementation, leaving it uncertain whether it is the program or the research that has failed.

The matter of statistically null results from program evaluation research deserves our close attention. Within the context of social programs and the policymaking that influences them, a null research finding is not merely an academic matter. Few program developers will greet with enthusiasm the claim that their program has no demonstrable effects nor will such programs readily escape the stigma that follows. Their funding, community and political support, and even survival may be negatively affected along with the morale of the program personnel themselves. Perhaps even more serious, the cumulation of erroneous evaluation studies can misdirect public policy and undermine support for whole categories of program initiatives that may in fact be genuinely effective (see Prather and Gibson, 1977).

Finally, we have to consider the long range implications for the evaluation research profession itself. How long will it be possible to engage routinely in weak, narrow research that potentially misrepresents program effects and still maintain credibility with the policy community? As policymakers and program administrators come to learn the limitations and deficiencies of evaluation research as now practiced under the experimental paradigm, their reaction may well be to condemn the whole approach, even when it is well done. Neither social programs, policymakers, nor evaluation researchers themselves are well served by the present ubiquity of feeble implementations of diluted versions of the experimental paradigm.

The lesson we draw from our analysis is that it is time to acknowledge that, despite its current widespread use, the experimental paradigm is not an all-purpose program evaluation methodology. Research under that paradigm requires special circumstances, resources, skills, and a time frame that permits appropriate attention to the details of design, measurement, treatment implementation, and program theory. The exacting nature of this kind of program evaluation research may, in fact, require that it become a largely academic endeavor. The usual demands for evaluation results that are timely and useful within the program setting may preclude the careful, systematic investigation of measures, treatments, and causes necessary to do good research under the experimental paradigm. Furthermore, the history of the most carefully conducted social intervention experiments (for instance, the negative income tax experiments) indicates that even after the evaluation results are reported they must be probed, criticized, and amended by the research community before their validity can be confidently judged.

This is not another polemic against use of the experimental paradigm in program evaluation nor a justification for some allegedly all-purpose alternate approach. It is rather an attempt to take seriously the requirements for valid experimental research under field conditions and avoid the embarrassment of invalid results when those requirements are not met. Our recipe for improving evaluation practice, therefore, is this: Do experimental research under circumstances where causal effects are a paramount issue and the methodological and conceptual requirements for good research can be met. Nothing will improve our general understanding of social programs and the principles of intervention in the social ecology faster than vigorous, causal, theoretically thoughtful, and methodologically sound experimental research. However, in circumstances where causal issues are not paramount or where it is not possible to do good experimental research, some alternative approach outside the experimental paradigm should be chosen in contrast to the current practice of conducting an impoverished, potentially misleading, and intrinsically uninterpretable version of experimental research.

This is not the place to discuss in detail the alternatives to the experimental paradigm that are available, but impressive cases have been made for the insight and understanding of social programs that can be gained through such approaches as studying program process, case flow, service delivery, and so forth in a program monitoring or information system mode (Attkisson and others, 1978), naturalistic observational and survey studies (Guba and Lincoln, 1981), and other such rational-empirical investigations (Cronbach, and others, 1980; Glass and Ellett, 1980; Scriven, 1974). These approaches are generally superior to the experimental paradigm for answering a broad range of important questions about social programs, many of which cannot be handled well within the experimental paradigm.

Eventually, it may be wise to distinguish between program research, which will draw on the power of the experimental paradigm for careful explication of the causal links and theoretical propositions embodied in social programs, and program evaluation, which will use less restrictive approaches to provide prompt, useful information to policy makers and program administrators about the specific programs with which they are concerned. By its very nature, program research may not be amenable to routine application under circumstances where answers are needed quickly or where support for extensive programmatic research is not feasible. And, by its nature, program evaluation may not be capable of answering the ultimate causal question, "Does this social intervention produce the intended effects?" The challenge to the evaluation profession is to know the difference between these approaches and their domains of applicability.

## References

Aiken, L. R., "Note on Sensitivity: A Neglected Psychometric Concept." *Perceptual and Motor Skills,* 1977, *45,* 1330.
Attkisson, C. C., Hargreaves, W. A., Horowitz, M. J., and Sorensen, J. E. (Eds.). *Evaluation of Human Service Programs.* New York: Academic Press, 1978.
Bernstein, I. N., and Freeman, H. E. *Academic and Entrepreneurial Research.* New York: Russell Sage, 1975.
Boruch, R. F., and Gomez, H. "Measuring Impact: Power Theory in Social Program Evaluation." In L. Datta and R. A. Perloff (Eds.), *Improving Evaluations.* Beverly Hills, Calif.: Sage, 1979.
Campbell, D. T., and Erlebacher, A. E. "How Regression Artifacts in Quasi-Experimental Evaluations Can Mistakenly Make Compensatory Education Look Harmful." In J. Hellmuth (Ed.), *Compensatory Education: A National Debate.* (Vol. 3). *Disadvantaged Child.* New York: Brunner/Mazel, 1970.
Campbell, D. T., and Stanley, J. C. *Experimental and Quasi-Experimental Designs for Research.* Chicago: Rand McNally, 1966.
Carver, R. P. "Two Dimensions of Tests: Psychometric and Edumetric." *American Psychologist,* 1974, *29,* 512-518.

Chen, H-T., and Rossi, P. H. "The Multi-Goal, Theory-Driven Approach to Evaluation: A Model Linking Basic and Applied Social Science." In H. E. Freeman and M. A. Solomon (Eds.), *Evaluation Studies Review Annual.* (Vol. 6). Beverly Hills, Calif.: Sage, 1981.

Chen, H-T., and Rossi, P. H. "Evaluating with Sense: The Theory-Driven Approach. *Evaluation Review,* 1983, *7,* 283–302.

Cohen, J. *Statistical Power Analysis for the Behavioral Sciences.* New York: Academic Press, 1977.

Cook, T. D., and Campbell, D. T. *Quasi-Experimentation: Design and Analysis Issues for Field Settings.* Chicago: Rand McNally, 1979.

Cronbach, L. J., and Associates. *Toward Reform of Program Evaluation: Aims, Methods, and Institutional Arrangement.* San Francisco: Jossey-Bass, 1980.

Glass, G. V., and Ellett, F. S. "Evaluation Research." *Annual Review of Psychology,* 1980, *31,* 211–228.

Gordon, G., and Morse, E. V. "Evaluation Research." In A. Inkeles, J. Coleman, and N. Smelser (Eds.), *Annual Review of Sociology.* Palo Alto, Calif.: Annual Reviews, 1975.

Guba, E. G., and Lincoln, Y. S. *Effective Evaluation.* San Francisco: Jossey-Bass, 1981.

Light, R. J. "Introduction." In R. J. Light (Ed.), *Evaluation Studies Review Annual.* (Vol. 8). Beverly Hills, Calif.: Sage, 1983.

Lipsey, M. W. "A Scheme for Assessing Measurement Sensitivity in Program Evaluation and Other Applied Research." *Psychological Bulletin,* 1983, *94,* 152–165.

Prather, J. E., and Gibson, F. K. "The Failure of Social Programs." *Public Administration Review,* 1977, *37,* 556–564.

Reichardt, C. S. "The Statistical Analysis of Data from Nonequivalent Group Designs." In T. D. Cook and D. T. Campbell, *Quasi-Experimentation: Design and Analysis Issues for Field Settings.* Chicago: Rand McNally, 1979.

Rutman, L. *Planning Useful Evaluations: Evaluability Assessment.* Beverly Hills, Calif.: Sage, 1980.

Scriven, M. "Evaluation Perspectives and Procedures." In W. J. Popham (Ed.), *Evaluation in Education: Current Applications.* Berkeley, Calif.: McCutchan, 1974.

Sechrest, L., and Redner, R. *Strength and Integrity of Treatments in Evaluation Studies. Evaluation Reports:* Washington, D.C.: National Criminal Justice Reference Service, 1979.

Sechrest, L., West, S. G., Phillips, M. A., Redner, R., and Yeaton, W. H. "Some Neglected Problems in Evaluation Research: Strength and Integrity of Treatments." In L. Sechrest, S. G. West, M. A. Phillips, R. Redner, and W. H. Yeaton (Eds.), *"Evaluation Studies Review Annual.* (Vol. 4). Beverly Hills, Calif.: Sage, 1979.

Sechrest, L., and Yeaton, W. H. "Empirical Bases for Estimating Effect Size." In R. F. Boruch, P. M. Wortman, and D. S. Cordray (Eds.), *Reanalyzing Program Evaluations.* San Francisco: Jossey-Bass, 1981.

Sechrest, L., and Yeaton, W. H. "Magnitudes of Experimental Effects in Social Science Research." *Evaluation Review,* 1982, *6,* 579–600.

Weiss, C. H. *Evaluation Research: Methods of Assessing Program Effectiveness.* Englewood Cliffs, N.J.: Prentice Hall, 1972.

Wholey, J. S. "Evaluability Assessment." In L. Rutman (Ed.), *Evaluation Research Methods: A Basic Guide.* Beverly Hills, Calif.: Sage, 1977.

Wortman, P. M., and Yeaton, W. H. "Synthesis of Results in Controlled Trials of Coronary Artery Bypass Graft Surgery." In R. J. Light (Ed.), *Evaluation Studies Review Annual.* (Vol. 8). Beverly Hills, Calif.: Sage, 1983.

Yeaton, W. H., and Sechrest, L. "Critical Dimensions in the Choice and Maintenance of Successful Treatments: Strength, Integrity, and Effectiveness. *Journal of Consulting and Clinical Psychology,* 1981, *49,* 156–167.

*Mark W. Lipsey is professor of psychology at Claremont Graduate School. He has conducted evaluations of juvenile delinquency treatment and a variety of other human service programs. His recent work focuses on methodological issues in program evaluation.*

*Scott Crosse is an evaluator in the Program Evaluation and Methodology Division at the U.S. General Accounting Office, Washington, D.C. He is also a doctoral candidate in the Department of Psychology at Claremont Graduate School. (The statements and opinions expressed in this chapter do not represent official U.S. General Accounting Office policy.)*

*Jan Dunkle is staff development coordinator for Charter Oak Hospital, a medical care facility in Covina, California. She is also a doctoral candidate in the Psychology Program at Claremont Graduate School.*

*John Pollard is a doctoral candidate in the psychology program at Claremont Graduate School. He has conducted research on counseling services and is currently interested in evaluation methodology and program theory.*

*Gordon Stobart is a doctoral candidate in the psychology program at Claremont Graduate School. He has recently completed a study of the social interaction of mainstreamed learning disabled children in the public schools.*

*There are numerous micro-level methods decisions associated with planning an impact evaluation. Quantitative synthesis methods can be used to construct an actuarial data base for establishing the likelihood of achieving desired sample sizes, statistical power, and measurement characteristics. Improvements in both primary and meta-analysis studies will be necessary, however, to realize the full potential of this approach.*

# Quantitative Synthesis: An Actuarial Base for Planning Impact Evaluations

*David S. Cordray*
*L. Joseph Sonnefeld*

In planning an evaluation, the decision to use a case study, a survey, or an experimental design depends on the nature of the question to be addressed. This concept is so fundamental that the Evaluation Research Society explicitly organized its *Standards for Program Evaluation* around the contingent nature of planning and execution decisions (see Rossi, 1982). As a simple illustration, if the evaluative question requires a numerical estimate of the impact of an intervention, it is generally agreed that the most defensible choice is a research design that meets high statistical standards, for example, a randomized experiment.

For most evaluation specialists, these determinations about design (macro-level planning decisions) are relatively straightforward. Once a particular approach has been selected (for example, a comparative study), however, there are numerous design features that must be considered that are pertinent to measurement, sample size, selection and assignment rules, timing of the postintervention assessment, and so on. We refer to these concerns as micro-level planning decisions.

As we proceed with this level of planning, we rely on experience, procedures used by others, collective wisdom (for example, advisory panels), common sense, or blind guesses to fill in the operational details. If we assess the state of the art in evaluation (see, Lipsey and others, this volume) as an indication of how successful micro-level planning has been in the past, it becomes clear that some remedial attention is warranted.

As a step towards improving the micro-level planning process, Cordray and Orwin (1983) have argued that quantitative synthesis methodology (for example, meta-analysis) can be used to facilitate some aspects of planning for new research and evaluations. The basic argument is quite simple: by systematically examining various products of the synthesis process (for example, effect sizes, attrition rates, and power coefficients), we can obtain an actuarial base for making projections of what we might expect to occur in future assessments. The purpose of this chapter is to provide a more comprehensive argument, focusing on strengths and limitations, for reliance on this type of observational evidence as a means to augment planning decisions in evaluation.

## Uncertainty in the Planning Process

When considering the usefulness of prior evaluation performance, it is beneficial to examine some of the decisions and sources of uncertainty that develop during the planning process. In particular, we will examine some of the decisions associated with planning an impact evaluation. This example has been adapted from a research proposal developed at the Center for Health Services and Policy Research (CHSPR) at Northwestern University (Hughes, Michell, and Cordray, 1983).

*Planning a Clinical Trial.* The proposed evaluation entailed a multi-site clinical trial aimed at assessing the effects of an intervention on the length of hospital stay (LOS) of selected Medicare patients within one of ten diagnosis related groups (DRGs). The intervention was conceived as a package of psycho-social services that were to be introduced within twenty-four hours after the patient was admitted. The key distinction between the proposed intervention and customary practices was the deliberate early initiation of the services.

Following conventional wisdom on staging social experiments (see Riecken and Boruch, 1974), approximately three months were devoted to determining the feasibility of implementing the intervention and the trial. After establishing that there existed sufficient interest, administrative support, and staff to introduce the intervention, attention was directed to stipulating more precisely the operational plan for the experiment. In particular, the guiding question was "How long will the experiment have to be conducted?" The answer to this question has obvious implications for staff allocations, budgets, timeliness, and ultimately quality of the evaluation. In determining the duration of the trial several critical factors had to be considered: the size and characteristics of the patient load, patient flow through the hospitals, magnitude of the effect, expected fidelity of the treatment, strength of the treatment, and various technical issues regarding the desired level of power and the sensitivity of the measures. Information had to be drawn from numerous sources.

Available administrative records provided some of the information, including:

- The number of beds in each site ranged from 389 to 451;
- The typical daily census was about 300 to 330 patients (a 73 to 77 percent occupancy rate);
- The average length of stay was between eight and eleven days;
- Not all of the patients were eligible for Medicare; only two of the three hospitals maintained statistics on their Medicare patients. Over the previous twelve month period, their average LOS was twelve to fourteen days;
- For the ten DRGs of interest, yearly patient caseload was available in two sites; average LOS for these groups was available in only one site.

Given the lack of complete information for each site, we made the reasonable assumption that data from the two sites could be used to estimate characteristics of the third site where information was completely absent. Armed with at least partial information from the administrative records (and willing to make leaps of faith), it appeared that roughly 1970 patients had been hospitalized under one of ten relevant DRGs during the previous twelve months. If we assumed that the patient admissions were evenly distributed across the year (only summary information was available), approximately 160 patients could be expected to be admitted in a hypothetical month—about fifty to fifty-five per site.

Since administrative records are primarily designed for accounting purposes, they were of little use in determining a central feature of the planning decision—the magnitude of the expected difference between those who were to receive the early intervention and those who were not. To estimate this parameter, the research literature was consulted. Boone, Coulton, and Keller (1981) reported a 1.25 day reduction in LOS for orthopedic patients who received comprehensive social work services in an urban acute care hospital. However, this study did not report a standard deviation. Using a standard deviation of 5.0 derived from Lindeman and Van Aernam (1971), we calculated a standardized effect size of .25 (1.25/5.0 = .25). Conventional statistical power analysis (Cohen, 1977) specifies that we would need 225 patients per group to detect a difference of this magnitude (power established at .80, alpha at .05, and employing a one-tailed test). Thus, a total of 450 patients would be needed for the trial.

Given the patient flow, estimated to be 150 to 165 per month across the three sites, the intervention would have to be in operation about three months to achieve the necessary sample size. With this simple calculation, we are assuming that no problems will be encountered (that is, all patients will cooperate fully, all will be eligible, and so on)—a dubious assumption. The power assessment should be agumented to account for known sources of patient loss. Our previous work suggested that not all patients (or their families, physicians, or friends) would consent to being part of the intervention (or control group). Some may be deemed ineligible due to risk considerations; others will not complete the post treatment assessment due to attrition or mortality. The magnitude of these postsolicitation losses, however, are difficult to estimate. Relying on a prior study (Hughes, Cordray, and Spiker, 1984), we estimated pretreatment refusal rate at 30 percent. Further, postassignment attrition from measurement, treatment, or true mortality was assumed to be, at most, 20 percent. Making adjustment to account for these losses resulted in a new estimate of ninety patients per month across the three settings. Specifically, if only 70 percent of the 160 patients per month were willing and eligible to participate, the available pool would be 114 patients. If 20 percent of these individuals failed to complete all phases of the study, then 80 percent of 114, or ninety patients would be included in the final assessment each month. At that rate, the trial would have to be in place five months rather than three.

These considerations rescue the design from a potential statistical power shortage. However, the sources of loss are unlikely to be random and may not be equivalent in structure across groups. Assessing the influence of these potential sources of selectivity bias entails an additional cost consideration—the need to measure attributes of those who decline, leave, and complete the trial. This entailed planning to assess 750 individuals, only 450 of whom would actually be included in the treatment conditions. While this increased the scope of the evaluation effort, the rationale for expanding the design was to reduce the ambiguities associated with departures (nonparticipation) from ideal experimentation conditions.

For the seasoned planner, using all available evidence (administrative records, prior studies conducted by others, prior experience, and intuition) in specifying an evaluation design is an obvious mechanism to achieve as close a match as possible to the realities of the situation (see Riecken and Boruch, 1974). How well this has worked in the past is open to speculation. We can get an idea of the potential for success by examining the knowledge base used in this example.

Single studies were used to derive estimates of the likely level of particular research factors (effect size) or problems (refusals). The estimate of attrition level was simply an educated guess. The extent to which these estimates are representative of the specific situation is unknown; they may have little value as a basis for planning. One way to refine these determinations is to broaden the knowledge base. We used quantitative synthesis methodology to expand and strengthen our planning decisions.

### Features of Quantitative Synthesis

The major part of our argument rests on the unique methodological characteristics of quantitative synthesis. The main features of this method are discussed below. (More detailed treatments of the process appear in Glass, McGaw, and Smith, 1981, Hunter, Schmidt, and Jackson, 1982, Light and Pillemer, 1984, and U.S. General Accounting Office, 1983.)

Quantitative synthesis is a generic methodological approach to summarizing prior evidence contained in primary studies. Its most distinctive features include: (1) the statistical transformation of results from primary studies into a common metric (that is, a standardized difference among treatment conditions—such as Cohen's $d$ statistic), (2) a statistically based aggregation of the results of primary studies, and (3) systematic examination of the characteristics of the study. The most popular version of quantitative synthesis is meta-analysis, introduced by Glass (1976).

Conceptually quantitative synthesis methods are simple and appealing. Six steps are typically involved. The first two steps—a clear specification of the questions of interest and an enumeration of the substantive domains of interest—are critical. For example, our domain may be all evaluation studies that were conducted on a particular program. This second step is similar to the delineating the population frame in survey research.

The third step—data gathering—is not unlike the more traditional literature review. Here the analyst conducts an extensive literature search covering published and unpublished reports pertaining to a given substantive domain. The primary objective is to identify the complete population of relevant studies that have been conducted. It should be obvious that what studies are gathered depends on how broadly (all studies) or narrowly (limited to impact studies) the domain has been specified in the earlier steps.

Step four is possibly the most time consuming component of the synthesis process. Each of the reports must be reviewed and information extracted. Typically, three types of information are recorded. These include: (1) the primary results or outcomes (effect sizes, probability levels, and test statistics); (2) information on the methodological characteristics of the study (assignment rules, attrition levels, sample sizes, and statistical power); and (3) study characteristics (contextual, participant, programmatic, and theory related dimensions). To date, the majority of attention has been directed at methods for extracting information on study outcomes.

The fifth step involves the actual synthesis process. One of the objectives of quantitative synthesis is to derive an overall estimate of the effects of an intervention strategy across multiple independent assessments. One method that has gained considerable appeal is to simply calculate an average effect size across assessments. Hedges (1981, 1982) has demonstrated the statistical pitfalls in such practices and provides some useful alternatives: (1) statistical procedures to test for the presence of heterogeneous estimates across a series of assessments, (2) adjustments for biases due to small samples, and (3) methods for calculating standard errors of estimates under a variety of statistical models. Rosenthal and Rubin (1982) also embellish conventional statistical theory as it applies to quantitative synthesis.

Hedges and Olkin (1983) illustrate several clustering techniques that could be performed once heterogeneity has been identified. Of course, the extent to which meaningful clusters (low versus high design quality) can be tested is dependent on how well the salient information that should be extracted to represent these factors has been specified in earlier steps. The analyst has the option of reexamining the studies for unrecorded characteristics; however, this is both time consuming and subject to the dangers of post hoc specification searches (see Leamer, 1978).

Having identified the clusters of studies to be summarized, the last step contains a variety of options for summarizing the results. The summary can be presented in various ways and some are more meaningful than others depending on the purpose of the synthesis. The two most popular presentation styles are the summary statistic format (an average effect size) and the tabular display (see Light and Pillemer, 1984). As we argue later in this chapter, both formats may be necessary to derive maximum utility from a quantitative synthesis.

*Implications for Planning Evaluations.* Many quantitative syntheses have been undertaken across a variety of substantive areas. The reports are almost exclusively devoted to the substantive topic under consideration. To date, little or no attention has been directed at the wealth of information that be collected (and sometimes is) on methodological features of the studies. Rather, this information is treated as a by-product of the synthesis process—information that is extracted while trying to account for differences in study outcomes. As we demonstrate, by examining information on the methodological underpinnings of prior studies, the utility of quantitative syntheses can be broadened beyond what they tell us about the effects of interventions. If properly conducted, these methodological assessments can represent an important resource for planning subsequent studies.

## Exploiting the By-Products of Quantitative Synthesis in Planning

The methodological characteristics reported as part of quantitative syntheses may provide an empirical basis for some critical front-end decisions. Hoaglin and others (1982) illustrate how assessments of the adequacy of research methods used to study the effects of medical interventions can support an argument for higher quality designs. Similarly, Soderstrom, Berry, and Hirst (1981) demonstrate how prior studies of the U.S. Department of Energy residential conservation initiatives can be used in planning subsequent studies. In both of these cases, the authors focus attention on the macro-level planning decisions, that is, choices among variations in designs. While useful in expanding or justifying methodological options, they do not provide evidence for the necessary microlevel considerations illustrated in our simple introductory example.

More appropriate to the level of detail needed to understand the constraints one is likely to encounter is the work reported by Heberlein and Baumgartner (1978), Andrews (1980), and Sudman and Bradburn (1974). Each of these authors has made substantial attempts to extract from a body of research very specific information on facets of the research process. Heberlein and Baumgartner (1978) go as far as providing prediction equations for estimating likely response rates to mail surveys. Of course, since these types of assessments are based on observational data the resulting models are easily subjected to misspecification errors (Cochran, 1982). Such criticisms, while technically accurate, miss the point of these exercises—a concern with reducing uncertainty in designing studies, not eliminating it.

If we consider the major attributes of the quantitative synthesis process—accumulation of all relevant studies, systematic recording of results and study characteristics, and tests to determine homogeneity of outcomes—we begin to see a way to avoid the selective use of individual studies as a basis for planning research. In our earlier discussion (Cordray and Orwin, 1983), we noted: "Systematic recording of research and treatment characteristics from this collection of studies provides a data base analogous to those used for estimating expectancies in actuarial tables. The basic notion is to establish a set of statistics that indicate the prevalence of specific research-related events. Just as insurance companies establish rates for premiums based on expected incidences, researchers can make their decisions on allocation of resources based on expectancies derived from previous research. The assumption here is that the sample of studies is at least representative of the variety of research conditions one would encounter in subsequent evaluations" (p. 98).

Returning to our example, recall that a pivotal piece of information for determining the duration of the clinical trial was the magnitude of the expected difference between the groups receiving the early social work intervention and those receiving it later. An estimate of this parameter was taken from a similar study (Boone and others, 1981). As noted, the representativeness of this study as an estimate of the population treatment effect parameter could be questioned on several grounds. For example, that study used orthopedic surgery patients, only half of whom received Medicare reimbursement. Our proposed study involved patients whose health condition was undoubtedly poorer.

To gain a broader base from which to judge the relative effects of the proposed intervention, a meta-analysis conducted by Mumford, Schlesinger, and Glass (1982) could be used. These researchers summarized thirty-four studies of the effects of psycho-social interventions on various measures of posthospitalization functioning. In all, 210 assessments were recorded from these studies. In an appendix to the paper, Mumford and others (1982) present some useful information on the characteristics of each study. This includes effect sizes for each measure, control group and experimental group sample size, research design (random, nonrandom, or unknown), and brief descriptions of the salient features of the treatment procedures and patient characteristics. As a means of illustrating how quantitative syntheses can be usad to facilitate planning decisions, the information reported by Mumford and others was reorganized following the cumulative likelihood notion described in Cordray and Orwin (1983).

Table 1 displays the observed effect size values across 210 assessments. We can readily see that the majority of values range between −.5 and +1.5, the modal effect size being 0.0. The cumulative likelihood values presented in the far right hand column simply summarize the relative likelihood of a given effect size ranging from low to high. This display provides an empirical basis from which to judge the relative likelihood of observing levels of standardized effects in future assessments.

The distribution of values in Table 1 provides more information than could be derived from summary statistics. Here, about 75 percent of the prior assessments have shown positive results (greater than or equal to +.1 ES). On the other hand, there appears to be a substantial chance of finding no difference or a negative effect of the intervention (roughly one in four). The latter should alert the analyst to the need for incorporating additional research design elements that distinguish between theory, program implementation, and method failures (see Lipsey and others, this volume; Yeaton, this volume). The cumulative likelihoods also indicate the range of plausible values that might be observed. Table 1 indicates that about half of the previous studies produced effects within the +.1 and +.8 range; the likelihood of observing ESs above 1.0 is only about one in ten.

In the planning example previously described, we employed an ES of .25. Judging from the assessments appearing in Table 1, this appears somewhat conservative. Over half of the prior assessments exceed this value. On the other hand, Table 1 contains multiple assessments (a total of 210) from each of the thirty-four studies. These include self ratings of psychological states (anxiety), ratings of medical progress, and level of postoperative care, as well as our primary measure of interest in the proposed clinical trial—reduction in LOS (length of stay). It is entirely reasonable to expect that different measures will produce substantially different effect sizes

Table 1. Cumulative Likelihood of Effect Size Values for Thirty-four Psycho-Social Interventions

| Recorded ES | | Cumulative Likelihood |
|---|---|---|
| <−.5 | XXXXX | .024 |
| −.4 | XXXX | .043 |
| −.3 | XXX | .057 |
| −.2 | XXX | .071 |
| −.1 | XXXXXX | .100 |
| 0.0 | XXXXXXXXXXXXXXXXXXXXXXXXXXXXXXXX | .252 |
| +.1 | XXXXXXXXXXXXXX | .324 |
| +.2 | XXXXXXXXXXXXX | .390 |
| +.3 | XXXXXXXXXXXXXXXXXXX | .481 |
| +.4 | XXXXXXXXXXXXXX | .548 |
| +.5 | XXXXXXXXXXXXXX | .619 |
| +.6 | XXXXXXXXXXXXXXXXXXX | .714 |
| +.7 | XXXXXXXXXXXXX | .781 |
| +.8 | XXXXXXXXXXXX | .843 |
| +.9 | XXXXXX | .871 |
| +1.0 | XXXX | .891 |
| +1.1 | XXXXXXXX | .933 |
| +1.2 | XX | .943 |
| +1.3 | XXXX | .962 |
| +1.4 | XX | .971 |
| +1.5 and above | XXXXXX | 1.000 |

*Source:* Adapted from Mumford, Schlesinger, and Glass, 1982.

*Note:* The total number of effect sizes equals 210 from thirty-four studies. These have not been adjusted for small sample biases (Hedges, 1981).

(see Cordray and Bootzin, 1983). A more precise use of the results of a synthesis would entail examining only those measures that are directly relevant.

A later meta-analysis conducted by Devine and Cook (1983) summarized sixty-two comparisons involving reductions in LOS. The actual LOS reductions, distribution, and cumulative likelihood values for this synthesis appear in Table 2. Looking at the LOS reductions reported for the sixty-two assessments, the magnitude of the effects in terms of actual reductions in days of hospitalization are reasonably homogeneous; nearly 70 percent fall between .51 and 1.50 days. About 13 percent of the studies show a null or negative affect of the intervention on LOS.

Even though the LOS measure is similar across assessments and does not need to be transformed into an ES for meaningful interpretation across studies, the effect size is useful when studies differ in terms of within-group variability. Devine and Cook (1983) reported both LOS reduction and ESs as part of their meta-analysis. The standardized LOS values (ESs) reveal a slightly different picture (see Table 3). Compared to the distributions in

Table 2. Cumulative Likelihood Levels of Reduction in Length of Stay (LOS)

| LOS Reduction | Distribution | Cumulative Likelihood |
|---|---|---|
| 0.00 or less | XXXXXXXX | .129 |
| .01 to .50 | XXXXXXXXXXX | .310 |
| .51 to 1.00 | XXXXXXXXXXXX | .500 |
| 1.01 to 1.50 | XXXXXXXXXXXX | .694 |
| 1.51 to 2.00 | XXXXXX | .790 |
| 2.01 to 2.50 | XXXX | .855 |
| 2.51 to 3.00 | XXXXX | .935 |
| 3.01 to 3.50 | | .935 |
| 3.51 or more | XXXX | 1.000 |

Source: Adapted from Devine and Cook, 1983.

Note: Based on a total of sixty-two assessments. For three assessments information was not available; a total of thirty-four studies were included in this meta-analysis.

Table 1, which contain many types of outcomes, the effects for LOS (alone) are more homogeneous. As before, the +.25 ES value derived from the single study appears to be somewhat conservative; over 50 percent of the prior assessments produced ESs that were higher.

*What Have We Learned?* Using the Devine and Cook (1983) meta-analysis results, we might be tempted to alter our judgment on the magnitude of the expected effect. Rather than .25, it seems plausible that the value could be as high as +.5 (45 percent of the prior studies were +.5 or larger). Consulting Cohen (1977), the necessary sample size for (each group) to detect a difference this large is 50; a 78 percent reduction over the initial estimate of 225 per group. Using the same estimates to adjust the monthly case load for suspected sources of pre- and postassignment attrition, the trial would have to be conducted for roughly a month and a half.

On the other hand, recall that the intervention to be tested represented a minor variation on the current hospital policy regarding social work services. That is, the new intervention simply amounted to early (within twenty-four hours) initiation of services. Interviews with administrators at one site revealed that the majority of patients in the target DRGs received social work care under normal hospital procedures. Since the proposed comparison would not entail a no treatment condition, we could expect the contrasting effect of early intervention to be small. Given this constraint, a conservative value seems appropriate unless all prior studies also contained weak treatments of this sort. This wrinkle points up the importance of knowing what types of treatments, comparisons, and participants are included in the body of prior research and evaluations. We return to this issue in the final section of this chapter.

*Is There More to Be Learned from Quantitative Synthesis?* The example presented earlier adjusted for various forms of patient loss. We assumed that

Table 3. Cumulative Effect Sizes for LOS in
Psycho-Social Interventions

| Effect Size | Distribution | Cumulative Likelihood |
|---|---|---|
| <−.5 |  | .000 |
| −.3 |  | .000 |
| −.2 | XXX | .055 |
| −.1 | XX | .091 |
| 0.0 | XXXX | .164 |
| .1 | XXX | .218 |
| .2 | XXXXXX | .327 |
| .3 | XXXXXX | .436 |
| .4 | XXXXXX | .545 |
| .5 | XXXXXXXX | .691 |
| .6 | XXX | .745 |
| .7 | XXXX | .818 |
| .8 | XX | .855 |
| .9 |  | .855 |
| 1.0 | XX | .890 |
| 1.1 | X | .919 |
| 1.2 | XX | .945 |
| 1.3 | XXX | 1.000 |
| 1.4 |  |  |
| 1.5 or more |  |  |

*Source:* Adapted from Devine and Cook, 1983.

*Note:* The total number of effect sizes equals fifty-five; for ten assessments there was insufficient information to calculate the effect size. Thirty-four studies were included in the meta-analysis. The effect sizes have not been adjusted for small sample biases (Hedges, 1981).

the particpation rates would be relatively high (for instance, 70 percent preassignment acceptance and eligibility and 80 percent postassignment retention throughout the duration of the trial). Data on these issues were not available from Mumford and others (1982) or Devine and Cook (1983). (See Cordray and Orwin for an illustration using the Smith, Glass, and Miller, 1980, psychotherapy meta-analysis). Both analysts do report evidence on the sample sizes used in the studies summarized; this provides some useful indirect information from which to judge the plausibilty of achieving a sample of a given size as determined in the a priori power analysis.

Mumford and others (1982) report the sample size for both the experimental and the control groups for each study they summarized. Table 4 shows that one-third of the studies used fewer than forty individuals, two-thirds used less than sixty, and only four of thirty-six (11 percent) involved sample sizes in excess of one hundred. These figures hint at a potential problem—there may simply be too few individuals in any given setting to participate in a study. If we assume that prior researchers are conscientious about a priori power assessments and these values appearing in Table 4 are

Table 4. Total Sample Sizes and Cumulative Likelihoods in
Psycho-Social Interventions

| Total Reported Sample Size | Frequency Distribution | Cumulative Likelihood |
|---|---|---|
| 1–20 | | 0.00 |
| 21–40 | XXXXXXXXXXXX | .33 |
| 41–60 | XXXXXXXXXXXX | .67 |
| 61–80 | XXXXXX | .83 |
| 81–100 | XX | .89 |
| 101–120 | | .89 |
| above 120 | XXXX | 1.00 |

*Source:* Adapted from Mumford, Schlesinger, and Glass, 1982.

*Note:* The total number of assessments equals thirty-six.

the product of attrition, refusal, and limited number of participants, then the prospects of conducting a statistically sensitive assessments in the future seems bleak unless substantial corrective actions, additional resources, and longer time frames are considered.

*Combining Information.* The cumulative likelihood columns in previous tables focus on individual design features of each assessment or study. The planning process can be sharpened considerably by examining multiple facets simultaneously. Table 5 presents salient features from nine randomized trials used in the Mumford and others (1982) meta-analysis. The studies are ordered according to the magnitude of the difference between groups. Four of the nine between-group differences are statistically significant, although seven reveal raw differences that are large enough to be considered meaningful. Contrasting the sample size (total) with the raw difference or effect size values reveals no consistent trend (some relatively small sample sizes produce significant differences, others do not, and the same is true for the studies with larger sample sizes). The last column of Table 5 reports estimates of the within-group standard deviations for these studies. As can be seen, there is substantial variability in this index across studies. In addition, the first study, with a sample size of 515, is actually composed of data from eleven individual sites. Expanding the number of sites to overcome inadequate samples sizes in one setting is a viable option that could be considered.

For planning purposes, it is essential to diagnose the sources of error that contribute to the size of the within group variability. When sample sizes are likely to be small due to the unavailability of participants or effects are expected to be small due to the strength or integrity of the intervention (see Yeaton, this volume), making provisions to minimize the size of the variance is a means of increasing the sensitivity of the overall design. Unfortunately,

Table 5. LOS Reduction, Sample Size, Estimated Pooled Standard Deviation, and Effect Sizes in Nine Randomized Designs

| Study | Raw Difference | S.E. | Total Sample | Effect Size | Standard Deviation |
|---|---|---|---|---|---|
| 1 | −.59 | .43 | 515 | −.15 | 4.88 |
| 2 | −.09 | .50 | 69 | −.05 | 2.08 |
| 3 | −.05 | .45 | 176 | −.02 | 3.00 |
| 4 | .89 | .69 | 30 | .30 | 1.83 |
| 5[a] | 1.01 | .50 | 64 | .54 | 2.00 |
| 6[a] | 1.91 | .62 | 261 | .34 | 5.00 |
| 7[a] | 2.10 | 1.07 | 50 | .55 | 3.78 |
| 8 | 2.40 | 1.43 | 70 | .23 | 5.98 |
| 9[a] | 2.70 | 1.06 | 97 | .67 | 5.22 |
| Wgt Average | .61 | | | .12 | |
| Average | 1.14 | | | .27 | |

Source: Adapted from Mumford, Schlesingar, and Glass, 1982.
Notes: S.E.= standard error of estimate.
[a] statistically reliable differance.
Standard deviations were estimated given available data.
Effect sizes not adjusted for small sample biases.

little information is available from meta-analyses to provide guidance in this area.

*Measurement Considerations.* With the exception of Hunter, Schmidt, and Jackson (1982), meta-analysts have directed little attention at extracting information on the psychometric properties of measures, subject heterogeneity, degraded measurement due to field administration conditions, and other sources of error. One exception is the synthesis of validity coefficients reported by Stanovich, Cunningham, and Feeman (1984). While not a meta-analysis, these researchers attempted to determine the magnitude of reported correlations among measures of reading ability and intelligence. They obtained ninety-five assessments (across grade levels and gender) appearing in the recent literature. In Table 6, these coefficients have been reorganized to display the distribution and cumulative likelihood of various levels of observed correlation among measures of these constructs. In general, across grade/age clusters the distribution of validity coefficients is quite symmetrical about the range of .46 to .50. Also, the magnitude of the validity coefficients seems to be related to the age/grade cluster of the individuals involved. Of course, if additional information (such as, reliabilities of each test and evidence of restricted range) were extracted in addition to these validity coefficients, this type of assessment would have more diagnositic value to the evaluation planner.

Table 6. Distribution of Validity Coefficients for
Reading Ability and Intelligence Scales

| Coefficient Range | Distribution[a] | Cumulative Likelihood |
|---|---|---|
| .01–.05 | | .00 |
| .06–.1 | | .00 |
| .11–.15 | | .00 |
| .16–.20 | 133 | .03 |
| .21–.25 | | .03 |
| .26–.30 | 223X | .07 |
| .31–.35 | 111112X | .15 |
| .36–.40 | 1122233 | .22 |
| .41–.45 | 11111122233XX | .36 |
| .46–.50 | 1111112333XXX | .50 |
| .51–.55 | 111112XXY | .59 |
| .56–.60 | 11112223XXXXXX | .74 |
| .61–.65 | 223XXXXXXXXYY | .86 |
| .66–.70 | XXXXXY | .93 |
| .71–.75 | 23Y | .96 |
| .76–.80 | 2X | .98 |
| 81 or more | XY | 1.00 |

*Source:* Adapted from Stanovich, Cunningham, and Feeman, 1984.

[a] 1 = Grade 1
  2 = Grade 2
  3 = Grade 3
  X = Grades 4–8
  Y = Grades 9 and above

*Notes:* The cumulative likelihoods are based on ninety-five assessments. Girls and boys were calculated separately, multiple coefficients were reported when multiple tests were utilized. See original article for additional breakdowns.

## New Directions and Redirections

The purpose of this chapter was to present an argument for more considered use of evidence about prior evaluation methodology and practices. We have argued that this information could serve to inform micro-level planning decisions for subsequent evaluations. While there are numerous ways to use the results of prior studies, our focus has been on the products of quantitative synthesis. The rationale for this emphasis stems from the unique methodological character of this mode of inquiry. That is, this approach attempts to gather the entire pool of relevant published and unpublished studies, systematically examines the methodological, substantive, and contextual features of the studies, and, through transformation of study outcomes into a common metric, provides a means of aggregating results, examining factors related to outcomes, and identifying the most promising (relatively speaking) interventions. Of course, the extent to which this perspective is actually helpful in planning future studies remains to be seen.

Whether or not anyone applies these notions in their planning process depends on a number of factors, including subsequent practices in research synthesis. In this summary section, we identify areas where synthesis practices could be improved and describe additional areas for exploration.

*The Status of Meta-Analysis and Related Synthesis Activities.* Meta-analysis and other forms of quantitative synthesis have become popular within the past decade. Shortly after Glass (1976) outlined the general tactics for summarizing evidence across studies, a series of critiques appeared. For some researchers (Eysenck, 1978), meta-analysis was viewed as an unsatisfactory approach to understanding the cumulative effects of interventions. These claims (combining apples and oranges, ignoring qualitative information, and the like) and counter claims are well known. Judging from the character of more recent commentary on the quantitative synthesis process, the research community appears to have moved from skepticism to cautious acceptance. Rather than hostile attacks, the recent commentary (see Bullock and Svyantek, 1985; Orwin and Cordray, 1985; Slavin, 1984) addresses ways of improving synthesis practices.

*Are All Studies Included?* Obtaining a universe of relevant studies was a principal justification for calculating the relative likelihood values for levels of study characteristics (attrition, effect sizes, and power coefficients). As with any research procedure that summarizes in statistical terms an array of information, a critical question is the extent to which all relevant elements (studies) have been included. There are diagnostic tests to determine the potential influence of omitting studies from the meta-analyses (the file drawer problem: Orwin 1983; Rosenthal, 1979), but the problem of developing an analogue for the omission of study characteristics is much less tractable (if at all).

On the other hand, we treat the relative likelihood distributions as advisory, imperfect aids for complex decisions. The bias, if any, in relying on a partial picture of prior practices would suggest that we use conservative, mid-range, likelihood values in making our planning decisions.

*Are all Effects Included?* So far the literature has been concerned with the exclusion of studies; an equally serious question is the exclusion of within-study effects. The meta-analyst has considerable latitude in determining which of many effects (measures and comparisons) to include in the data base. For example, Orwin and Cordray (1985) report deriving nearly twice the number of effects as reported by Smith, Glass, and Miller (1980). Accounting for this selectivity is a much more difficult problem than the publication biases and the file drawer issues and an area requiring further attention.

*Following Good Research Practices.* The utility of quantitative synthesis depends on the soundness of the procedures employed in gathering, summarizing and reporting tha evidence. With few exceptions, analysts have ignored even the simplest notions of sound research practice. For example, estimates of the reliablity of the data coding process are rarely computed (or at least rarely reported). The obvious problem for users of the synthesis (whether for substantive or planning purposes) is that unreliable coding introduces additional noise into an already noisy system of inquiry. The noise created by unreliable coding turns to bias when multivariate statistical procedures are employed to examine differences among classes of interventions (see Orwin, this volume).

For planning subsequent evaluations based on evidence collected from prior assessment, unreliability results in uncertainty. For example, Mumford and others (1982) and Devine and Cook (1983), mentioned earlier, both examine the effects of psychosocial interventions on the postoperative length of stay in hospitals. While these meta-analyses differ in important ways, they do rely on an overlapping set of studies. In contrasting the coded values reported by each set of authors, we noticed substantial agreement, but there were also some important inconsistencies in how studies were categorized. Of the ten studies included in both meta-analyses, for instance, both sets of authors agreed that the assignment process was either random or nonrandom in eight studies. But Devine and Cook decided that two studies entailed nonrandom assignment while Mumford and associates classified these as random. Inconsistancies in the derived effect size calculations were also apparent in four of the twelve results that are reported for the overlapping estimates. Whether these errors average out is unclear. If more reliance is placed on the distribution of values extracted from prior research studies, quality control mechanisms such as those proposed by Trochim (this volume) seem to be an important step towards maximizing the utility of these summaries.

*Deficient Reporting.* The problems associated with coding are partly due to the nature of observational data and partly attributable to the poor reporting practices of primary researchers. Mosteller, Gilbert, and McPeek (1980) view the latter as a sufficiently important issue to warrant publishing recommendations to editors and researchers on the type and extensiveness of information that should be reported for clinical trials. Orwin (this volume) offers other solutions.

*Research Characteristics: General or Specific?* Looking across various meta-analyses at the variables used to characterize the quality of the research, rarely more than a handful of indicators were employed. These may include ratings of internal validity, categorization of the reactivity of measures, specification of sample sizes and postassignment attrition levels, degree of experimental blinding, method of participant assignment, and type of comparison. To date, there has been little attention devoted to articulating what technical factors should be included in assessments of prior research and evaluations. Notable exceptions are the rating schemes developed by Chalmers and others (1981), U.S. General Accounting Office (1978), Hoaglin and others (1982) and Mosteller and others (1980). For the most part, these checklists are general and simply require summary judgments. To make information about research quality more useful requires dividing summary judgments into their constituent parts. For example, the statistical power of a comparison can be summarized as a single value. More diagnostic, however, would be evidence on the component parts, that is, the raw difference between groups, within group variability, measurement sensitivity, sample size, and measurement error. If, in planning a particular study, sample sizes must be restricted, a sensible alternative is to devote attention to other components that influence the sensitivity of the design (for example, matching prior to assignment, devising more sensitive measures, and enhancing the strength of the intervention). Exercising these options intelligently depends on a detailed understanding of prior successes and failures.

*Quantitative and Qualitative Evidence.* In our scheme, both quantitative evidence and qualitative descriptions are essential if planning decisions are to be reasonably well tailored to a particular situation. Reducing a complex design, treatment, or set of participant characteristics to numerical values probably obscures as much as it illuminates. As such, narrative descriptions are a necessary component of the synthesis process. For example, by looking at the descriptions of clients in the studies summarized by Prioleau, Murdock, and Broady (1983), Cordray and Bootzin (1983) conclude that the studies represent a highly select type of clientele (school-age children) and the results may not be applicable to another population of interest. Rather than belabor this point, the reader is referred to thoughtful discussions of the role of "numbers and narrative" appearing in Cook and Leviton (1980) and Light and Pillemer (1984).

*Capitalizing on the Substantial Efforts of Reviewers.* In our discussion of the phases of the synthesis processes, we stated that the most time consuming aspect was reading and recording information. Our principal message is that these efforts can be made more rewarding by recognizing that many of the resulting details can be put to good use in planning subsequent evaluations. To facilitate this, however, authors and editors will need to see the value of devoting journal space to more complete descriptions of studies, and quantitatively oriented reviewers will have to make the details of their coding readily available to the research and evaluation community. The material that we have used in generating our examples in this paper are the product of exemplary practices in these regards.

With reduced federal support for interventions and evaluation, it is necessary that we maximize the quality of those studies that are undertaken. Gaining a normative base from which to make planning decisions may facilitate these efforts. Some may claim we have oversimplified the planning process—that programs are too unpredictable to warrant extensive investments in detailed planning. On the other hand, it may be that we have not taken a sufficiently hard enough look at the uncertainty we impose when we plunge in without first taking stock of the rich history of successful and unsuccessful practices.

## References

Andrews, F. "Measuring the Quality of Measurement: Estimates from Structural Modeling Techniques." Invited address, American Psychological Association, Montreal, Canada, Sept. 4, 1980.

Boone, C. R., Coulton, C. J., and Keller, S. M., "The Impact of Early and Comprehensive Social-Work Services on Length of Stay." *Social Work in Health Care,* 1981, 7(1), 1–9.

Bullook, R. J., and Svyantek, D. J., "Analyzing Meta-Analysis: Potential Problems, an Unsuccessful Replication, and Evaluation Criteria." *Journal of Applied Psychology,* 1985, 70(1), 108–115.

Chalmers, T. C., Smith, H., Jr., Blackburn, B., Silverman, B., Schroeder, B., Reitman, D., and Ambroz, A. "A Methodology for Assessing the Quality of Randomized Control Trials." *Controlled Clinical Trials,* 1981, 2, 31–49.

Cochran, W. G. *Planning and Analysis of Observational Studies.,* New York: Wiley Interscience, 1982.

Cohen, J. *Statistical Power Analysis for the Behavioral Sciences.* New York: Academic Press, 1977.

Cook, T. D., and Leviton, L. C. "Reviewing the Literature: A Comparison of Traditional Methods with Meta-Analysis." *Journal of Personality,* 1980, 48, 449–472.

Cordray, D. S., and Bootzin, R. R. "Placebo Control Conditions: Tests of Theory or Effectiveness." *The Brain and Behavioral Sciences,* 1983, 2, 286–287.

Cordray, D. S., and Orwin, R. G. "Improving the Quality of Evidence: Interconnections Among Primary Evaluations, Secondary Analysis, and Quantitative Synthesis." In R. J. Light (Ed.), *Evaluation Studies Review Annual.* (Vol. 8). Beverly Hills, Calif.: Sage, 1983.

Devine, E. C., and Cook, T. D. "Effects of Psycho-Educational Interventions on Length of Post-Surgical Hospital Stay: A Meta-Analytic Review of Thirty-four Studies." In R. J. Light (Ed.), *Evaluation Studies Review Annual.* (Vol. 8). Beverly Hills, Calif.: Sage, 1983.

Eysenck, H. J. "An Exercise in Mega-Silliness." [Comment]. *American Psychologist,* 1978, 33, 517.

Glass, G. V. "Primary, Secondary, and Meta-Analysis of Research." *Educational Researcher,* 1976, 5, 3–8.

Glass, G. V., McGaw, B., and Smith, M. L. *Meta-Analysis in Social Research.* Beverly Hills, Calif.: Sage, 1981.

Heberlein, T. A., and Baumgartner, R. "Factors Affecting Response Rates to Mailed Questionnairas: A Quantitative Analysis of the Published Literature." *American Sociological Review,* 1978, 43(4), 447–462.

Hedges, L. V. "Distribution Theory for Glass's Estimator of Effect Size and Related Estimators." *Journal of Educational Statistics,* 1981, 6, 107–128.

Hedges, L. V. "Estimation of Effect Size from a Series of Independent Experiments." *Psychological Bulletin,* 1982, 92, 359–369.

Hedges, L. V., and Olkin, I. "Clustering Estimates of Effect Magnitude from Independent Studies." *Psychological Bulletin,* 1983, 93(3), 363–573.

Hoaglin, D. C., Light, R. J., McPeek, B., Mosteller, F., Stoto, M.A. *Data for Decisions; Information Strategies for Policymakers.* Cambridge, Mass.: Abt Books, 1982.

Hughes, S. L., Cordray, D. S., and Spiker, V. A. "Evaluation of a Long-Term Home Care Program." *Medical Care,* 1984, 22(5), 460–475.

Hughes, S. L., Michell, W., and Cordray, D. S. *Evaluation Proposal: A Multi-Site Assessment of the Impact of Early Social Work Services.* Unpublished proposal, Center for Health Services and Policy Research, Northwestern University, Evanston, Illinois, 1983.

Hunter, J. E., Schmidt, F. L., and Jackson, G. B. *Meta-Analysis: Cumulating Research Findings Across Studies.* Beverly Hills, Calif.: Sage, 1982.

Leamer, E. E. *Specification Searches: Ad Hoc Inference with Nonexperimental Data.* New York: Wiley, 1978.

Light, R. J., and Pillemer, D. B. *Summing Up: The Science of Reviewing Research.* Cambridge, Mass.: Harvard University Press, 1984.

Lindeman, C. A., and Van Aernam, B. "Nursing Intervention with the Presurgical Patient: The Effects of Structured and Unstructured Preoperative Teaching." *Nursing Research,* 1971, *20,* 319–332.

Mosteller, F., Gilbert, J. P., and McPeek, B. "Reporting Standards and Research Strategies for Controlled Trials; Agenda for the Editor." *Controlled Clinical Trials,* 1980, *1,* 37–58.

Mumford, E., Schlesinger, H. J., and Glass, G. V. "The Effects of Psychological Intervention on Recovery from Surgery and Heart Attacks: An Analysis of the Literature." *American Journal of Public Health,* 1982, *72*(2), 141–151.

Orwin, R. G. "A Fail-Safe N for Effect Size." *Journal of Educational Statistics,* 1983, *8,* 157–159. Doctoral Dissertation, Northwestern University, Evanston, Illinois, 1982.

Orwin, R. G., and Cordray, D. S. "Effects of Deficient Reporting on Meta-Analysis: "A Conceptual Framework and Reanalysis." *Psychological Bulletin,* 1985, *97*(1), 134–147.

Prioleau, L., Murdock, M., and Brody, N. "An Analysis of Psychotherapy vs. Placebo Studies." *Brain and Behavioral Sciences,* 1983, *4,* 1–30.

Riecken, H. W., and Boruch, R. F. (Eds.) *Social Experimentation: A Method for Planning and Evaluating Social Interventions,* New York: Academic Press, 1974.

Rosenthal, R. "The 'File Drawer Problem' and the Tolerance for Null Results." *Psychological Bulletin,* 1979, *86,* 638–641.

Rosenthal, R., and Rubin, D. "Comparing Effect Sizes of Independent Studies." *Psychological Bulletin,* 1982, *92,* 500–504.

Rossi, P. H. (Ed.). *Standards for Evaluation Practice* New Directions for Program Evaluation, no.15. San Francisco: Jossey-Bass, September, 1982.

Slavin, R. E. "Meta-Analysis in Education: How Has it Been Used?" *Educational Researcher.* 1984, *13,*(8), 6–15.

Smith, M. L., Glass, G. V., and Miller, T. I. *The Benefits of Pychotherapy.* Baltimore, Md.: Johns Hopkins University Press, 1980.

Soderstrom, J., Berry, L., and Hirst, E. "The Use of Meta-Evaluation to Plan Evaluations of Conservation Programs." *Evaluation and Program Planning,* 1981, *4,* 113–122.

Stanovich, K. E., Cunningham, A. E., and Feeman, D. J. "Intelligence, Cognitive Skills, and Early Reading Process." *Reading Research Quarterly,* 1984, *19*(3), 278–302.

Sudman, S., and Bradburn, N. M. *Response Effects in Surveys: A Review and Synthesis,* Chicago, Ill.: Aldine Publishing Co., 1974.

U.S. General Accounting Office. *Evaluation Synthesis.* Washington, D.C.: U.S. General Accounting Office, Institute for Program Evaluation, 1983.

U.S. General Accounting Office. *Assessing Social Program Impact Evaluations: A Checklist Approach.* Washington, D.C.: U.S. General Accounting Office, Program Analysis Division, 1978.

*David S. Cordray is group director for public assistance and federal evaluation policy in the Program Evaluation and Methodology Division at the U.S. General Accounting Office. He is on leave from Northwestern University. (The statements and opinions expressed in this volume do not represent official U.S. General Accounting Office policy.)*

*L. Joseph Sonnefeld is a doctoral candidate in the Division of Methodology and Evaluation Research at Northwestern University. He has conducted research and evaluations in juvenile justice, cross-cultural managerial training, and cognitive aspects of survey methodology.*

*Strength and integrity issues are central to the planning and interpretation of evaluative studies. In the absence of actual data from previous studies, estimates of strength and integrity can often be derived in other ways. These issues of strength and integrity are described in the context of resource allocation in evaluation research.*

# Using Measures of Treatment Strength and Integrity in Planning Research

*William H. Yeaton*

The purpose of this chapter is to argue that measures of treatment strength and integrity can be very useful in planning studies. The discussion naturally complements longstanding emphasis on the use of previous study outcomes in planning studies, as when estimates of effect size are utilized to set desired sample size. Particular attention will be paid to methodological and conceptual issues surrounding measures of treatment strength and integrity. Guidelines will be provided to assist the reader in estimating treatment strength and integrity in the absence of actual data from previous studies. Numerous examples will be cited to demonstrate ways in which strength and integrity can be measured and these measures related to treatment outcomes. Some of the potential pitfalls one may encounter in conducting and interpreting these measures will be presented. Finally, the value of such measures will be discussed as a specific solution to the general problem of resource allocation in evaluation research.

## Why Are Measures of Treatment Strength and Integrity Important?

Measures of treatment strength and integrity are particularly important because they inform other decisions with regard to planning research. For example, if previous studies suggest that strength and integrity are likely to be relatively low, one might buttress the sensitivity of planned outcome measures. Lipsey (1983) has provided a scheme for assessing measurement sensitivity in the evaluation area. His analysis suggests that by choosing particularly sensitive measures or by combining several measures to improve reliability, statistical power can be enhanced. A researcher unaware of potentially low treatment strength and integrity might not consider the need to use more sensitive outcome measures. Thus, knowledge of treatment strength and integrity can impact the statistical conclusion validity and minimize the likelihood of Type II errors.

Measures of treatment strength and integrity also allow the researcher to make stronger inferences regarding effects produced. For example, in the face of a difference between treatment and no-treatment groups, measures of treatment integrity would allow one to attribute the difference to the presence of treatment in the treatment group and the absence of treatment in the no-treatment group (assuming other explanations of difference in the two groups have been controlled). Without knowledge of the degree of actual treatment implementation in the treatment group and the lack of treatment in the no-treatment group, one cannot say that it is the treatment that accounts for differences. In the face of a no-difference finding, lack of knowledge regarding treatment implementation leaves open the possibility that findings are due to the unintended absence of treatment in the treatment group or the presence of treatment in the no-treatment group.

Knowledge of treatment strength and integrity provides valuable information about the mechanism of change relating treatment and outcome. If researchers have a clear understanding of the dimensions of treatment that lead to potential change (that is, the active elements of treatment from which judgments are made regarding strength), then knowledge of the integrity of these dimensions allow stronger statements about those elements of treatment functional to change, what Cook and Campbell (1979) call construct validity of cause.

From this somewhat brief discussion it appears that measures of strength and integrity may be particularly advantageous, both in terms of the independent research decisions that are informed and the ways in which such decisions enhance the validity of research. Despite these advantages, however, relevant information regarding strength and integrity is seldom provided (Yeaton, 1982). One can offer numerous reasons to account for the dearth of strength and integrity measures in the evaluation literature despite previous arguments for their inclusion (Cook and Poole, 1982; Sechrest and others, 1979). Hopefully, by articulating the value of measures of strength and integrity, by offering several instances of their appropriate use, and by outlining some of the pitfalls users may encounter, this chapter will encourage such use.

## Strength and Integrity: Initial Considerations

While the notions of treatment strength and integrity are not new to the evaluation community, Sechrest (Sechrest and Redner, 1979) has been instrumental in its rekindled interest to the evaluation community. Until this time, most of the literature on treatment strength and integrity has addressed the importance of these factors in enhancing the intrinsic value and interpretability of research, but their utility in planning subsequent studies has not yet been emphasized.

*Strength: A Definition.* Strength refers to the a priori likelihood that a treatment would have its intended effect. The use of the term *a priori* in the definition suggests that strength assessments are made before knowledge of outcomes, though in actual practice, prior knowledge of outcome may influence determinations of strength. Drug analogues nicely illustrate intuitive notions of strength. For example, aspirin is a strong treatment for headache, though perhaps not for a migraine, and certainly not for sinus congestion.

*Implementing Strong Treatment.* Strong treatments, generally speaking, would be preferred over weak treatments (there are exceptions, however; see Yeaton and Sechrest, 1981b, for examples), but we may not always be able to have the luxury of maximizing treatment strength. Rossi and Lyall (1976), in their book on the negative income tax (NIT) experiment, discuss the notion of policy space as a range of values that are likely to be of interest to decision makers. Subsidies provided to the unemployed at two to three times the poverty level represent treatments that most persons would consider quite strong. However, the maximum level actually used in the NIT study was 125 percent of the poverty level since higher levels were judged to be politically and financially unrealistic. Likewise, there will often be practical and ethical constraints on the allowable choices of treatment strength open to researchers. Values from outside of this range may be judged unacceptable to potential consumers of treatment (Kazdin, 1981) and are likely to seriously compromise external validity. Thus, we must carefully assess the implementability of treatments in judging desirable levels of treatment strength.

*Integrity: A Definition.* Integrity concerns the extent to which a treatment is implemented as intended. This definition infers that there is an explicit goal, a level of treatment implementation to which the researcher aspires. It also implies that at least some general means exist for assessing treatment, even if those means are only that treatment was or was not implemented as intended. Again using the NIT experiment as an example, if participants who were supposed to receive income subsidies did not in fact receive them or perhaps received them after the scheduled date, treatment integrity has been compromised.

*Implementing Treatments with High Integrity.* There is an interesting precedent that may prove quite useful in establishing desired levels of treatment integrity in the planning stages of research, namely the notion of tolerance in the manufacturing of precision tools. Specification of machine parts must be correct within some tolerated error, the degree of tolerance being generally dependent on the risk of falling outside the range. For a neurosurgeon there will be little room for deviation. The same might be true of psychological interventions with suicidal patients. For other cases, deviation may be acceptable. In the same way that the need for fallback designs should be anticipated in the event that the preferred design cannot be implemented, so too should fallback procedures be available in the event that initial efforts to maintain treatment integrity cannot be maintained.

There are important considerations that may constrain the degree to which factors influencing integrity are under the researcher's control. For example, in the medical field a distinction is often made between the efficiency and effectiveness of medical technologies (Office of Technology Assessment, 1978). Efficiency refers to the results of studies conducted under ideal conditions of implementation, that is, high in treatment integrity, while effectiveness refers to results found in applications of the technology for which treatment integrity is likely to be compromised. These two kinds of studies ask different questions and emphasize different types of validity. Efficiency probes the maximum effect that can be expected and tends to emphasize internal validity while effectiveness sheds light on the kinds of results likely to be found in applications of the technology and therefore emphasizes external validity.

An analogous continuum exists between theoretical and applied research. Theoretical research is likely to be carefully controlled, often being conducted under analogue conditions. Typically, it is criticized as lacking in external validity, the very dimension that applied research touts as its strength. The point is that the question being addressed will dictate the degree to which researchers are free to alter variables that maximize treatment integrity. For example, just as steps could be taken to minimize the threat of differential attrition (for example, by paying respondents to complete long term follow-up questionnaires), so too could steps be taken to ensure treatment integrity (for example, by returning monetary deposits from persons in smoking cessation studies who have completed all assigned tasks). However, the relevance of such steps to maximize integrity in planning research will depend on the applied or theoretical nature of the experimental question.

*Relationship Between Strength and Integrity.* Conceptually, treatment strength and integrity are independent. Both strong and weak treatments can be implemented at high and low levels of integrity. In practice, though, departures from planned treatments will likely weaken these treatments. Thus, in the discussion regarding treatment integrity that immediately follows, a more realistic assumption is that a relationship exists between treatment integrity and strength.

It is quite likely that plans to enhance treatment strength may alter treatment integrity and vice versa. For example, treatment packages have been offered as a means of increasing strength under the premise that some element of treatment will be especially pertinent to each person (Baer, 1977). However, the resulting increase in treatment complexity may make it difficult to maintain treatment integrity. Similarly, efforts to maximize treatment integrity may impact treatment strength. Maintaining extensive monitoring systems to measure integrity may have adverse effects on providers (as well as being so reactive that bias results), reducing their general enthusiasm and motivation to administer the program.

*Implicit Measures of Strength and Integrity in the Absence of Data.* As noted above, explicit measures of treatment integrity from previous studies may not be available to the researcher interested in planning. There are, however, several sources within a given research context that are likely to be associated with inconsistent treatment implementation. For example, the greater the number of different treatment providers included in a study, the more likely that treatment implementation will vary. The same can be said of the number of settings in which treatment is given—multiple settings are likely to be associated with multiple versions of treatment. If the treatment is to be implemented again and again over a considerable period of time, the precise manner of implementation is very likely to drift, even if a single provider administers treatment.

It is interesting to note that the above factors—multiple providers, multiple settings, and extended time periods—are precisely those that are present in multi-center clinical trials in medicine (see Lipids Research Clinics Program, 1984). The field of medicine's response to potential treatment degradability is the development of a detailed protocol whose purpose is to ensure consistently implemented procedures. While the use of a treatment protocol (and a strategy for monitoring its implementation) would maintain the integrity of treatment, this feature has not been routinely adopted by evaluation researchers.

The nature of the treatment itself may also be a source of inconsistent implementation. Those treatments that are high in complexity are likely to be easily degraded. Drug treatments often represent a kind of integrity dichotomy—persons either take two aspirin or they do not. In contrast, there are many elements to a surgical procedure and each can be implemented to different degrees. The same can be said of psychotherapies, though different surgeries as well as different psychotherapies will vary in their complexity.

There are also likely to exist contextual and publication contingencies that will predict the level of integrity to be expected. The presence of the research team may be associated with relatively high integrity levels since providers may be motivated to follow precise treatment specifications to please researchers. So too would settings in which intake and scheduling have been routinized for some time. Publication contingencies that favor difference findings would lead to the predition that researchers use their influence to see that treatments are adhered to.

*Relationship Between Strength and Integrity and Treatment Outcome.* Careful thought should also be given to assumptions that the researcher holds with regard to the relationship between strength or integrity and the outcomes of treatment. If one makes the simplistic assumption that the realtionship is linear, efforts to increase strength or integrity by $x$ units will result in treatment outcomes being altered by $y$ units. A more realistic assumption might be that the shape of the relationship is nonlinear. Efforts to enhance strength or integrity at some parts of the curve will result in relatively more or less change in treatment outcome. There may well be flats in the curve— ranges over which increasing strength or integrity produce no change in outcome. In fact, the relationship may not be monotonic, as when stronger treatments produce lower levels of outcome (Caplan, 1968).

At the very least, one should acknowledge the possibility of marginal benefits in efforts to increase strength or integrity—the additional effort required to produce bigger outcomes may be expensive in both time and money. If the world is assumed to be complicated, it can be expected that the strength and integrity of different treatments would be differentially related to outcomes or that the strength and integrity of a given treatment may be related differently to outcomes at different periods of time.

## Measuring Strength and Integrity

Measures of treatment strength and integrity can be utilized in a number of ways to assist in the planning of research. In the examples that follow, numerous suggestions are offered and, in some cases, data are provided. Some methods of relating strength and integrity measures to treatment outcomes are also included. These examples are supplemented with discussion of pitfalls to be avoided in measuring strength and integrity and in relating these measures to treatment outcomes.

*Using Ratings by Experts.* One of the ways in which treatment strength can be measured capitalizes on the knowledge of experts within a particular substantive field. Presumably, experts are skilled in assessing strength by virtue of their familiarity with the theory that relates particular interventions to their effects. Thus, their familiarity with the likely casual mechanism of change and their ability to determine the extent to which these casual mechanisms are present within a given study argue that experts' a priori assessments of strength should be quite consistent with actual treatment outcomes.

To test this speculation, seventeen Fellows of Division 8 (The Division of Personality and Social Psychology) of the American Psychological Association were given brief descriptions of treatments found in five different studies of the *Journal of Personality and Social Psychology* (Sechrest and Yeaton, unpublished). These experts were asked to judge the strength of the treatment as described and to estimate the average score on the dependent variable in the experimental group. Not only did these experts have little trouble providing estimates of strength, but when these estimates were compared to the actual manipulation check values reported in the five studies, the average of the seventeen correlations obtained was .76. An even larger correlation of .84 was obtained when the average judge estimate was correlated with the actual manipulation check values. Thus, these data strongly suggest that the expertise of appropriate experts can be utilized to make an accurate a priori assessments of the strength of psychological treatments.

Similarly, experts were also requested to make a priori assessments of smoking treatments (Yeaton and Sechrest, 1981a). After reading capsulized descriptions of treatments taken from published studies, experienced researchers and practitioners predicted probable effects. When experts' predictions of the percent of patients who would stop smoking were correlated with the actual smoking cessation rates, the average correlation was .47. Some judges achieved correlations in the .70s. Again, experts proved to be quite capable of assessing treatment strength, at least as judged by eventual treatment outcomes. It is interesting to note that accurate estimates of the relationship between treatment strength and outcomes in the above two examples were made without knowledge of treatment integrity, information that would reasonably have raised the correlations.

*Using Previous Study Information.* The evaluation of a particular intervention for patients with coronary artery disease (namely, coronary artery bypass graft surgery—CABGS) provides an interesting context to illustrate how previous studies can yield valuable information regarding strength and integrity. CABGS is a procedure that grafts a portion of vein taken from the leg of the heart patient to bypass a diseased heart vein. The number of vein grafts used in the bypass procedure should directly reflect the increased proportion of oxygenated blood reaching the heart and thus could be thought of as a measure of treatment strength—the more clogged arteries bypassed, the stronger the treatment. Integrity of treatment is reflected in the degree to which an open conduit to the heart has actually been accomplished. Though patency of the graft is typically measured as a dichotomy (a graft is either patent or not patent), the percent of patients in the

## Table 1. Coronary Artery Bypass Graft Surgery (CABGS): Strength and Integrity Data

*Descriptive statistics* (N = 73 of 90 studies from Wortman and Yeaton, 1983)

|  |  | N | Min | Max | M | SD |
|---|---|---|---|---|---|---|
| P = | Patency rate (integrity variable) | 38 | 65.0 | 100.0 | 81.2 | 9.3 |
| N = | No. grafts/operation (strength variable) | 51 | 1.3 | 2.9 | 2.1 | 0.4 |
| % = | Percent mortality | 60 | 1.0 | 50.0 | 11.4 | 8.0 |

*Correlations*

|  | N | r= |
|---|---|---|
| (P, %) | 32 | −.08 |
| (N, %) | 40 | −.19 |

Key:  N = number of studies
 Min = minimum
 Max = maximum
 M = mean
 SD = standard deviation
 r = Pearson correlation

surgical group with patent grafts seems a reasonable proxy for treatment integrity—the greater the patency rate, the higher the integrity.

Using a previously published research synthesis as a source of data on treatment strength and integrity (Wortman and Yeaton, 1983), 73 of 90 studies were identified that reported either the number of grafts per operation or the graft patency rate (see Table 1). The average number of grafts per operation in 51 studies was 2.1 (standard deviation = 0.4), and the average patency rate in 38 studies was 81.2 (standard deviation = 9.3) during the period from 1970 through 1981.

In addition, one can examine the relationship between these strength and integrity variables and outcome by correlating these measures with mortality. As one might expect, each of these measures correlates negatively with mortality—the greater the number of grafts per operation and the higher the patency rate, the lower the rate of mortality in CABGS patients. While the correlations, −.08 and −.19, are small, probably due to the inconsistent presence and absence of other factors associated with mortality (for instance, the severity of the cardiovascular disease, the medical center in which the operation was performed), the example does illustrate how proxies for treatment strength and integrity can be measured and validated.

The author is in the final stages of a systematic review of the outcome literature on implosion therapy (Nurius and Yeaton, unpublished). Close inspection of the literature reveals that it is quite feasible to obtain information regarding treatment strength and integrity from previous studies. Two dichotomous variables in particular appeared to us to represent good proxy measures of treatment integrity. First, whether or not an implosion hierarchy had been established and, second, whether or not boundary conditions had been met. (Hierarchy refers to the stepwise manner in which anxiety-producing situations are introduced, while the boundary conditions criterion asks whether extinction has been achieved at each step of the hierarchy as required by the theory on which implosion is based.) Similarly, two dichotomous strength variables were commonly reported: whether or not the primary therapist had received a Ph.D. and whether or not homework sessions were part of the intervention. As in the example with CABGS, it is also possible to relate these strengths and integrity variables to the results of treatment. While we have not yet calculated these correlations, we would expect those studies that have established hierarchies and met boundary conditions or that have used Ph.D. therapists and assigned homework sessions to result in greater degrees of beneficial change than those studies for which treatment strength and integrity were relatively low.

*Caveats.* Given the relatively recent emphasis on treatment strength and integrity, it seems appropriate to offer some caveats to those researchers inclined to measure strength and integrity or relate them to treatment outcomes.

*Be Cautious of Strength and Integrity Measures Lacking Validity.* It is important to remember that strength and integrity measures, like all measures, may be deficient in traditional validity terms. Apparent validity can be achieved relatively easily, for example, by recording attendance of persons in training sessions. However, apparent validity alone is not sufficiently stringent as a criterion measure for treatment integrity. Issues of construct validity should be also considered to maximize the value of measures of treatment integrity.

*Avoid post hoc measures relating strength and integrity outcomes.* Another potential pitfall with measures of treatment integrity relates to the possible post hoc nature of the data. Mark (1983) has cautioned the evaluation community about the dangers of interpreting differences between groups displaying high and low levels of treatment integrity. It cannot be assumed that the only difference between such groups is their level of treatment integrity. Since self-selection has occurred, participants will almost certainly differ in terms of their motivation and need to receive treatment. Since the difference in self-selecting variables between high and low integrity groups is likely to be related to treatment outcomes, biased estimates of treatment effects will result and internal validity will be compromised in contrasts made between groups.

In the field of medicine, a similar caution has been aired by members of the Coronary Drug Project Research Group (1980). In a randomized, double-blind, placebo-controlled clinical trial, the primary purpose was to evaluate the effectiveness of several lipid-influencing drugs on cholesterol levels and mortality. Patients were partitioned into high and low adherence groups, and results indicated that high adherers had significantly reduced mortality. The researchers rightly suspected that self selection into the high and low adherence groups had produced differences in patient characteristics between subgroups. Attempts were made using multivariate statistical methods to adjust for baseline differences in the two adherence subgroups, but these efforts were unsuccessful. The authors concluded that "These findings and various other analyses of mortality in the clofibrate and placebo groups of the project show the serious difficulty, if not impossibility, of evaluating treatment efficacy in subgroups determined by patient responses. . . ." (p. 1040). Thus, post hoc measures relating treatment integrity to outcome, with or without statistical adjustment, are to be considered suspect.

*Beware Causal Inferences with Correlative Data.* In the CABGS and implosion examples discussed above, efforts were also taken to relate measures of strength and integrity to outcomes by using correlations as a measure of the relationship. Thus, all the usual shortcomings regarding correlative measures apply. Since the unit of analysis in each of these correlations is the study, or more precisely, a group within each study, there will be many confounding variables that may influence the correlations found. (For example, attrition from high and low integrity subgroups and relative length of follow-up would be critical in both examples.)

*Do not Correlate Strength and Integrity Measures with Effect Size.* Another problem likely to occur when one wishes to validate the importance of strength and integrity measures pertains to characteristics of the outcome measure rather than to aspects of the strength or integrity measure. In both the implosion and the CABGS examples, care was taken to relate strength and integrity measures to only those results in the treatment group. Relating these measures to an index such as effect size would be a serious mistake since the mean and standard deviation of the comparison group would influence the value of the effect size index. There is no apparent reason why the level of strength and integrity in the experimental group should be related to comparison group data. What one would expect when correlating strength and integrity measures with effect size is that the stronger the comparison group, the smaller the correlation. (Stronger comparison groups—in the same sense as stronger treatment groups—are those that share an increasing number of elements with the treatment group; placebo controls would be stronger than contact controls which would, in turn, be stronger than wait list controls). Cordray and Bootzin (1983) present a more complete discussion of this point, and Landman and Dawes (1982) provide quantitative estimates for placebo effect size.

## Using Information on Strength and Integrity to Efficiently Allocate Study Resources

In the first portion of this chapter, it was noted that information on treatment strength and integrity could inform other treatment decisions such as the choice among measures varying in sensitivity. In this section, the value of strength and integrity data will be placed in a still larger context, namely the allocation of fixed resources available to a researcher.

A particularly cogent illustration of the value of strength and integrity information relates to choosing a sample size likely to yield a statistically significant difference between experimental and comparison groups. Standard practice dictates that specific values of alpha, power, and effect size be used to enter tables such as those provided by Cohen (1977) in order to establish a sample size for the contrast groups of a study. Unfortunately, the novice researcher is not likely to factor treatment strength or integrity in the expected effect size. Stronger treatments could be expected to raise the mean of the experimental group while enhancing treatment integrity should reduce variability in the denominator of the effect size index. Both efforts will increase expected effect size and allow studies with fixed power to be conducted with much smaller samples. This advantage will be particularly important when participants are expensive (difficult to identify and recruit or expensive to encourage as participants). Should strong treatments be expensive (in the NIT experiment, relatively small increases in the size of subsidies would be greatly magnified by the number of participants involved under national policy directives), efforts to enhance treatment integrity become even more critical if total sample size is to be minimized.

To illustrate potential savings, consider a plan to conduct a study for which the results of two groups will be contrasted. Alpha is set at the usual .05 level, the power desired is .80, and the anticipated effect size is .30. In this case, 140 participants would be needed for each of two groups. However, if a somewhat stronger treatment were used that was implemented with greater integrity, then perhaps the effect size expected could be increased to .40. With the same alpha level and power, only 78 participants per group would be needed, a reduction of 44% in the sample size. Accordingly, the fixed time and money available to the researcher can be shifted away from identifying, recruiting, treating, and analyzing results of some 62 participants in each of two groups and allocated to other research activities (side studies, development of multiple measures, supplementary analyses) that would enhance the interpretability of the research.

## References

Baer, D. M. "Perhaps it Would Be Better Not to Know Everything." *Journal of Applied Behavior Analysis,* 1977, *10,* 167–172.

Caplan, N. "Treatment Intervention and Reciprocal Interaction Effects." *Journal of Social Issues,* 1968, *24,* 63–88.
Cohen, J. *Statistical Power Analysis for the Behavioral Sciences.* New York: Academic Press, 1977.
Cook, T. D., and Campbell, D. T. *Quasi-Experimentation: Design and Analysis Issues for Field Settings.* Chicago: Rand McNally, 1979.
Cook, T. J., and Poole, W. K. "Treatment Implementation and Statistical Power." *Evaluation Review,* 1982, *6,* 425–430.
Cordray, D. S., and Bootzin, R. R. "Placebo Control Conditions: Tests of Theory or Effectiveness?" *The Brain and Behavioral Sciences,* 1983, *2,* 286–287.
Coronary Drug Project Research Group. "Influence of Adherence to Treatment and Response of Cholesterol on Mortality in the Coronary Drug Project." *New England Journal of Medicine,* 1980, *303,* 1038–1041.
Kazdin, A. E. "Acceptability of Child Treatment Techniques: The Influence of Treatment Efficacy and Adverse Side Effects." *Behavior Therapy,* 1981, *12,* 493–506.
Landman, J. T., and Dawes, R. "Psychotherapy Outcome. Smith and Glass's Conclusions Stand Up Under Scrutiny." *American Psychologist,* 1982, *37,* 504–516.
Lipids Research Clinics Program. "The Lipid Research Clinics Coronary Primary Prevention Trial Results. I. Reduction in Incidence of Coronary Heart Disease. *Journal of the American Medical Association,* 1984, *251,* 351–364.
Lipsey, M. W. "A Scheme for Assessing Measurement Sensitivity in Program Evaluation and Other Applied Research." *Psychological Bulletin,* 1983, *94,* 152–165.
Mark, M. M. "Treatment Implementation, Statistical Power, and Internal Validity." *Evaluation Review,* 1983, *7,* 543–549.
Nurius, P. S., and Yeaton, W. H. "Anatomy of a Research Synthesis Review: Meta-Analysis of Implosion Therapy Research." Unpublished manuscript, Institute for Social Research, Ann Arbor, Mich.
Office of Technology Assessment. *Assessing the Efficiency and Safety of Medical Technologies.* Washington, D.C. Government Printing Office, 1978.
Rossi, P. H., and Lyall, K. C. *Reforming Public Welfare. A Critique of the Negative Income Tax Experiment.* New York: Sage, 1976.
Sechrest, L., and Redner, R. "Strength and Integrity of Treatments in Evaluation Studies." *Evaluation Reports.* Washington D. C.: National Criminal Justice Reference Service, 1979.
Sechrest, L., West, S. G., Phillips, M. A., Redner, R., and Yeaton, W. H. "Some Neglected Problems in Evaluation Research: Strength and Integrity of Treatments." In L. Sechrest, S. G. West, M. A. Phillips, R. Redner, and W. H. Yeaton (Eds.), *Evaluation Studies Review Annual.* (Vol. 4). Beverly Hills, Calif.: Sage, 1979.
Sechrest, L., and Yeaton, W. H. "Assessing the Strength of Treatments: Comparing Ratings of Treatment Strength and Manipulation Checks in Social Psychological Research," unpublished manuscript, Florida State University, Tallahasse.
Wortman, P. M., and Yeaton, W. H. "Synthesis of Results in Controlled Trials of Coronary Artery Bypass Graft Surgery:" In R. J. Light (Ed.), *Evaluation Studies Review Annual.* (Vol. 8). Beverly Hills, Calif.: Sage, 1983.
Yeaton, W. H. "A Critique of the Effectiveness of Applied Behavior Analysis Research." *Advances in Behavior Research and Therapy,* 1982, *4,* 75–96.
Yeaton, W. H., and Sechrest L. "Critical Dimensions in the Choice and Maintenance of Successful Treatments: Strength, Integrity, and Effectiveness." *Journal of Consulting and Clinical Psychology,* 1981a, *49,* 156–167.
Yeaton, W. H., and Sechrest, L. "Estimating Effect Size." In P. M. Wortman (Ed.), *Methods for Evaluating Health Services.* Beverly Hills, Calif.: Sage, 1981b.

*William H. Yeaton is assistant research scientist at the Center for Research on the Utilization of Scientific Knowledge at the University of Michigan. His research interests include evaluation research methodology and research synthesis.*

*Information that describes a program's implementation and client audience can help the evaluator tailor the study to the constraints of particular settings and increase the likelihood that the evaluation can be implemented as planned.*

# Using Program Information to Plan Evaluations

## Sherry Holland

Listing ways in which evaluation methods have improved in the past twenty years, Cook (1984) suggests that evaluators now ask a broader range of questions, use more varied techniques, better integrate evaluation into prior research, and take into account practical constraints identified by the first generation of evaluators. This chapter focuses on the last—using prior research to identify programmatic constraints on subsequent research. The premise is straightforward: Taking program information into account when planning evaluations should increase the likelihood that the evaluation can be implemented as planned and that the results can be interpreted and used.

The need to include more comprehensive and detailed information about programs in evaluations has been argued at length (see Cronbach and Associates, 1980). One way in which such information can be used is to improve the efficiency of established programs. Data describing program procedures and clients can help answer questions such as why certain targeted individuals participate in the program while others do not, why some program elements work well and others do not (Cook, 1984), or what treatment procedures work best for which types of clients (Light, 1984). Another way in which program information can be used is to gauge the likely effectiveness of a treatment in new settings. When relevant data are available, investigators can identify the active ingredients of treatment that must be included in the replication and estimate probable participation rates (Light, 1984).

The advantage of using program information to plan evaluations is less frequently discussed. The evaluation plan typically is shaped by theoretical and methodological concerns. The implementation of the plan, on the other hand, is constrained by local realities. For example, in planning the research the evaluator may conduct a statistical power analysis to estimate the size of the sample needed to detect an effect. In the field, the evaluator's achieved sample depends on amount of funding, participation rates, eligibility criteria, and so on. When the difference between the evaluation as planned and the evaluation as implemented is large, the utility of even the most politically relevant, theoretically significant, and methodologically sound study can be distressingly attenuated.

The central theme of this chapter is that descriptive information about the national program can be useful in identifying the likely constraints of the particular contexts in which the evaluation will take place. A summary of events across sites is also useful in interpreting site-specific data. Program information—for example, descriptive information about client characteristics, size and location of clinics, nature and quality of services provided, staff allocation—is routinely collected by monitoring agencies (for instance, the National Drug and Alcoholism Treatment Utilization Survey of the Department of Health and Human Services), and is often obtainable at relatively low cost from local projects. Access to such information when planning an evaluation can alert the evaluator to issues and specific questions that will be useful to the program as well as to program circumstances that will influence implementation of the evaluation. This point will be illustrated by using a national treatment data base and a specially conducted survey of local projects. First, however, program information will be defined in greater detail and placed within an integrative framework.

## A Framework for Describing Programs

Social programs are complex. Although program modeling is receiving increasing attention (Chen and Rossi, 1984), as yet there is little consensus about how to characterize and measure programs. Therefore, a framework for describing programs that identifies major components and some illustrative elements within those components will be provided.

The framework consists of three major components that can be represented by concentric circles (see Figure 1). In the innermost circle is "treatment," what is actually done to program recipients. In the next circle is what Chen and Rossi (1984) refer to as the "implementation system," or that which is required to deliver the treatment. In the outermost circle is the "environmental context," which places additional constraints on treatment-as-delivered and significantly affects treatment outcomes.

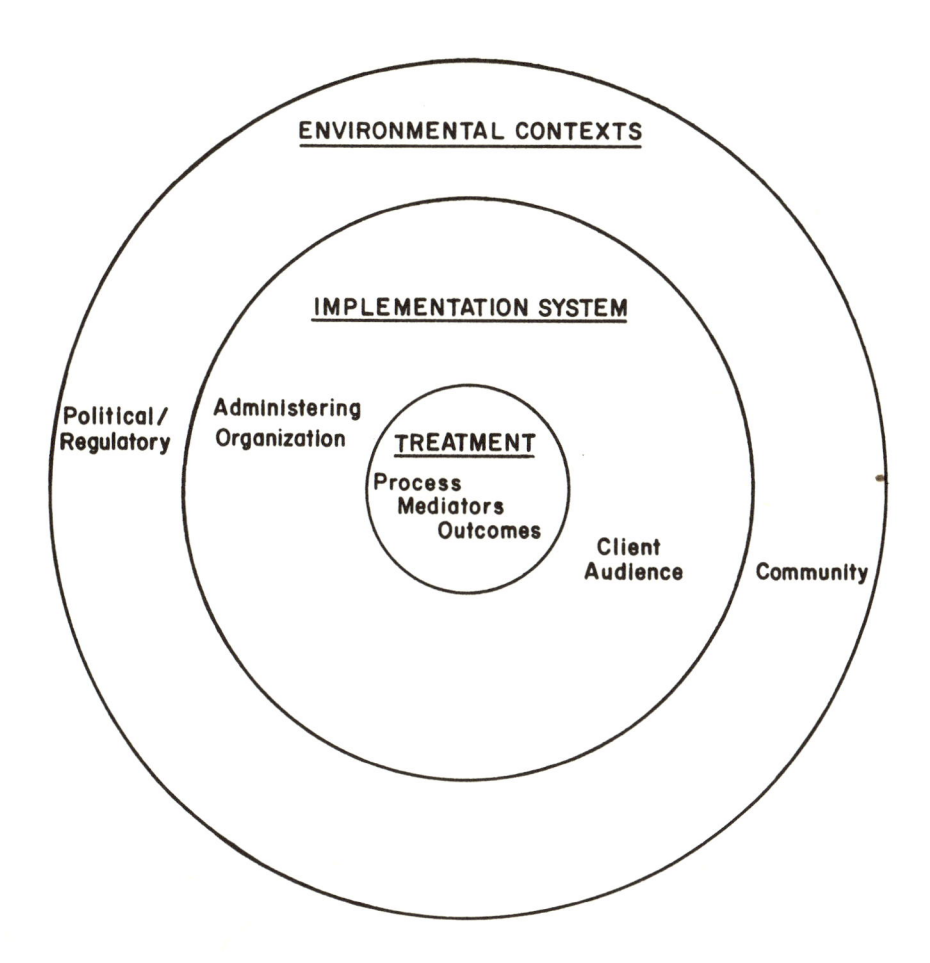

Figure 1. Simplified Schema of a Social Program.

[Diagram: Three concentric circles. Outer circle labeled ENVIRONMENTAL CONTEXTS (Political/Regulatory, Community); middle circle labeled IMPLEMENTATION SYSTEM (Administering Organization, Client Audience); inner circle labeled TREATMENT (Process, Mediators, Outcomes).]

*Treatment.* As Lipsey and others (this volume) note, treatment takes on various forms and levels of complexity (for instance, an educational curriculum, surgical procedure, or administrative change). However, even the simplest treatment consists of three classes of elements: process/input, mediating, and outcome variables.

Process/input variables are the activities, procedures, and techniques undertaken to produce particular effects. Process/input variables can be further specified as to nature and strength. For example, the treatment process in a drug treatment clinic could be described in terms of services (such as individual or group counseling), procedures (such as prescribing medication as part of the treatment plan), change induction techniques (such as modeling), and aspects of the treatment environment (Moos and Finney, 1983). Sechrest and Redner (1979) suggest parameters for assessing treatment strength, such as amount of treatment per unit of time (hours of individual or group counseling per week), size of the group, extent of participation of staff and clients, planned duration of treatment, and clarity of the treatment plan.

Mediating and outcome variables, or outputs, are the attitudes, cognitions, feelings and behaviors that are to be added to, changed, or eliminated from clients' repertoires. Planned or intended outcomes (goals) are distinguishable from actual or achieved outcomes. Mediating variables are those changes hypothesized to be necessary for persons to attain and maintain intended outcomes.

Causal theories relating inputs and outputs can be simple or complex. An early hypothesis relating methadone maintenance and criminality stated that, since drug abusers commit crimes in order to buy drugs, providing abusers with free drugs will eliminate criminal behavior. A more complex theory assumes that criminal behavior is multi-determined. Drug abusers commit crimes not only to buy drugs but also to buy food and clothes, to pay the rent, because it is acceptable (even normal) behavior within their reference group, because it is the only thing they know how to do, and because the individual finds criminal activity exciting (Lukoff, 1974). According to this theory, in order to eliminate criminal behavior it is necessary to change several mediating variables such as attitudes, job skills, and coping behaviors.

*Implementation System.* This component consists of two parts: an administering organization and a client audience. Specifically, an organization administers the resources necessary for providing treatment. It can be described in terms of variables such as size (client capacity, static or changing) cost (budgeted and actual), number and type of staff, years in operation (as a measure of degree of implementation), the nature of the physical facility, and administrative approach.

Clients are targeted to receive the treatment. It is assumed that clients vary in their response to treatment. They can be described in terms of social-demographic and diagnostic variables, criterion behaviors, treatment expectancies, and so on. They can also be characterized with respect to their movement in and out of treatment, such as rate of admission, completion rates, and posttreatment mortality. Some client variables interact with participation and completion rates, such as the availability of insurance to cover the cost of treatment, legal status, and availability of alternative housing.

*Environmental Context.* The final program component consists of two parts: the political regulatory context and the community context.

The political/regulatory context consists of the legislation (rules and regulations, funding agencies, competing programs, and the like) that defines and circumscribes what programs may do. For some programs it includes the client referral process. Funding sources are a key element in the political/regulatory context.

The community context consists of those factors that serve to maintain or negate treatment gains and otherwise influence client and program characteristics. The community can be described with respect to geographic location, population density, resources, and problems. Thus, a job training program may teach clients skills, but these people may be unable to get jobs if community unemployment rates are high. The community can also be described with respect to the nature of the client's relationship with the family or other support groups that may affect posttreatment functioning.

Consistent with current usage, a program is considered a national effort to ameliorate a social problem; projects, clinics, or sites are the entities within programs with direct responsibility for delivering treatment. The three-component descriptive framework presented here can be used to characterize the program at multiple levels, such as federal, regional, state, clinic. For example, the administering organization for the national program (for instance, a federal agency) has its staff, budget, and organizational personality as does the project's administering organization. Likewise, most of the descriptive elements referred to in this chapter make sense at multiple levels. A project's size can be described in terms of number of beds or clients treated during a period of time. Likewise, a national program's size can be described in terms of number of projects providing treatment or number of persons treated by the program. A construct such as "administrative approach" can refer to differences among states with respect to how they disseminate information to sites (St. Pierre and Cook, 1984), or to differences among projects with respect to how they communicate technical knowledge to front-line staff (Love, 1983).

## Using Program Information in Planning Evaluations

In its early formulation, evaluation researchers conceived of programs as treatment entities that were independent of an administering organization or setting (see Sells, 1972). Among the problems resulting from this approach was the inability to interpret differences in outcomes for similar treatments or to anticipate the probable impacts of the treatment in different settings. A central tenet of the current discussion is that program information is not only necessary for interpreting outcomes and estimating their generalizability, but also helps in designing better evaluations. To provide a case example, attention will focus on national drug abuse treatment programs and the issues relevant to their description and evaluation.

What, then, are some of the lessons we have learned and how can this knowledge be used to improve evaluations and programs? In their summary of the status of methadone maintenance treatment ten years after the initial experiment was disseminated nationally, Dole and Nyswander (1976) attributed the program's lackluster performance largely to political/regulatory and implementation problems. The treatment was perceived negatively by the public at large: "What was not anticipated . . . was the nearly universal reaction against the concept of substituting one drug for another, even when the second drug enabled the addict to function normally" (p. 2117). Controls imposed by federal and state agencies on clinics resulted in an environment inimical to treatment:

> With rigid rules mandating every detail of treatment and teams of inspectors from five or more separate agencies combing the records of clinics for technical violations, the physician is made to feel as defensive as the addicts and is left with no real authority in his clinic. He is told what addicts he is permitted to treat, the dosage limits and the permitted dose forms, the required frequency of clinic visits, what laboratory tests are mandated, the number and kinds of paraprofessional staff required for licensing of the clinic, and he must justify a decision to continue treatment of any patient after an arbitrary period of time (p. 2119).

The treatment was not accepted by sizeable numbers of the target population:

> . . .[T]he reason most often given by addicts for their rejection of treatment was their perception of cynical and uncaring attitudes in the staff of programs, unreasonable rules, rigidity, and lack of respect. . . . In addition, the misinformation continuously circulated by antimethadone agencies on the medical effects of methadone (gets in bones) is widely believed. In the past few weeks, a woman addict in jail, her veins obliterated and her body covered with ulcers from subcutaneous injections of contaminated heroin, was asked whether she would like to apply for a methadone program. Her answer was negative because she felt that methadone would be bad for her health (p. 2119).

Finally, the treatment theory had been oversimplified. Methadone alone was insufficient to effect targeted outcomes. At the very least, rehabilitation required "compassion and skillful counseling".

This capsule evaluation illustrates what has now attained the status of truism: treatment as originally conceived and as delivered in initial trials is not the treatment as delivered when expanded to other sites, nor is treatment by any name likely to be identical to treatment under a similar name in another setting. Treatments vary with respect to process and goals, and their success or failure depends on a large number of implementation and environmental factors. We are not concerned here with the debate on the relative importance of internal or external validity in evaluations. Our concern is more mundane; whether one views the elements in the implementation system and the environmental contexts as noise to be controlled in order to get a better estimate of the magnitude of the treatment effect or as necessary conditions for treatment success, these factors still need to be considered in any evaluation. Prior research, theory, and what we describe here as program data help evaluators identify those factors which may be associated with differential outcomes. Careful consideration of these factors when planning evaluations can increase the likelihood that the research can be conducted as planned, interpreted, and used.

## The Residential Drug Free Preassessment

An evaluation of residential drug free (RDF) treatment for drug abusers illustrates the use of program data in planning research. The evaluation was funded under the Title XX Donated Funds Initiative and was conducted between July 1980 and June 1981. While RDF is a generic label masking considerable variability in treatment-as-delivered, classical RDF treatment is community-based, incorporating a self-help model and structured to socialize residents to prosocial beliefs and attitudes and to shape patterns of productive behavior. Planned duration of the classical regimen is typically twelve to eighteen months. Available evidence suggests that length of stay is the single best predictor of positive outcomes (see Simpson, 1981; Holland, 1983).

The RDF evaluation was undertaken in anticipation of the shift from federal to state funding of drug prevention and treatment services under the Alcohol, Drug Abuse, and Mental Health Services Block Grant Program. While the change in the funding mechanism increased state funding flexibility, it also reduced the level of funding. State planners needed information about how to make optimal use of shrinking treatment resources. One strategy considered (a singularly procrustean solution) was to reduce the per-client cost of RDF treatment by reducing planned duration of treatment. Thus, a smaller number of long-term RDF slots (or budgeted beds) would be converted to a larger number of short-term slots.

To assist state planners and clinic administrators, the original evaluation plan called for a study of short-term treatment models. If RDF clinic administrators were going to have to modify current practices, they would need detailed information about what could be accomplished, with whom, by what means, and in what specified periods of time. State planners needed information about the relative cost effectiveness of short- and long-term treatment for different client types. Under the original plan, knowledgeable workers in the field would nominate exemplary short-term projects that would be studied in depth, and information about successful practices would be provided to planners and managers.

However, basic information necessary for an evaluation of short-term treatment was unavailable. Informants were unable to nominate exemplary short-term projects because they did not know the duration of treatment for familiar projects. Also, there was no consensus about how long short-term treatment was, or about how short-term treatment might differ from long-term treatment. Thus, the study shifted to what has been termed a preassessment (Hendricks, 1982). Making use of national program data collected by the federal treatment monitoring agency (the National Institute on Drug Abuse), supplemented by a specially conducted project survey, the evaluators obtained information about how projects function, their clientele, and treatment characteristics (such as duration) in order to plan the evaluation. They felt that a description of program implementation would aid in the planning process by providing them with an empirical basis for estimating the feasibility of conducting an impact evaluation, for giving rival explanations a probabilistic basis, and for identifying points of leverage within the program.

Data describing RDF clinics were obtained from the National Institute on Drug Abuse (NIDA). NIDA maintained a national treatment data base, National Drug and Alcoholism Treatment Utilization Survey (NDATUS), as well as a national client data base, Client Oriented Data Acquisition Project (CODAP). The NDATUS was conducted periodically until 1982 to describe the nature and distribution of drug abuse and alcoholism treatment in the United States. The 1980 NDATUS obtained information from 8,935 alcoholism and drug abuse projects. This included data on physical environment, client population served, unit ownership, services provided, and clients in treatment and budgeted capacity by modality and environment, unit staffing, and sources and amount of unit funding. A supplemental questionnaire developed for this study focused on organizational structure, client information, and information about the treatment process not available through NDATUS.

In the preassessment, data were collected in three stages. First, 884 projects were identified as potential providers of community-based (that is, non hospital) RDF treatment. Project staff were asked, by means of a screening letter, whether they provided RDF treatment and, if so the planned duration of treatment.

Second, extensive descriptive data for a subset of projects were requested from NIDA. This subset included non hospital projects that had responded to NDATUS, had provided information about duration of RDF treatment in the screening letter, and offered only one RDF option (N=448). Although clinics that provided more than one RDF option (for example, a three-month treatment regimen and a twelve-month treatment regimen) were of considerable interest, we were concerned that clinic staff would be unable to break out cost, client, and other information for the separate treatment options from their administrative records. Ultimately, data were obtained for 302 clinics from NIDA.

Third, the supplemental project questionnaire was sent to 120 clinics, a random sample of the 448 single-option clinics stratified by planned treatment duration: less than 6 months, 6 to 11 months, and 12 months and longer. Completed questionnaires were returned by 93 clinics (78 percent).

## Using Program Information to Plan Better Evaluations

*Sampling.* A fundamental use of information about projects in planning evaluations is to select possible sites for study. Even when sites are selected at random, a list of the sites that make up the program is required. However, as St. Pierre and Cook (1984) point out, selecting sites randomly is rarely reasonable. Rather, sites are usually selected purposively, to fulfill particular information needs and according to certain criteria. Purposive sampling entails identifying stratification criteria and deciding where to sample along the distribution of the stratification variables. Decisions about where to sample along the distribution are best made after inspecting the actual distribution of the program parameter. Thus, if one is interested in studying typical size sites, one needs to know the range and median of site sizes. Knowing the distribution of the variables across which one wishes to generalize also allows the evaluator to estimate the representativeness of the sample with respect to the population.

In an impact evaluation, one may wish to sample on the dependent variable to maximize the likelihood of detecting an effect. For example, in a current evaluation of a nursing intervention designed to reduce length of stay in hospital (Devine, O'Connor, and Wenk, 1985), the evaluators examined the distribution of average days in hospital for different surgical procedures. They targeted patients for study whose surgery typically required a median length of stay. At the low end of the distribution, the evaluators reasoned, length of stay was already so short that no treatment was likely to lower it further. At the high end of the distribution, long-stayers appeared to have medical problems in addition to those that precipitated the surgery that threatened to confound the effects of the treatment.

*Estimating the Likelihood That the Evaluation Can Be Implemented as Planned.* Slippage between evaluation as planned and evaluation as implemented can be expected in most studies and generally entails a series of design compromises. Estimating the feasibility of implementation is the link between the evaluation plan and its realization. This link can be strengthened by basing estimates of achieving targets on prior information. We will illustrate this point using national summary information about project size, resources, and procedures.

When the unit of analysis is the individual respondent, research reports frequently read like "The Case of the Disappearing N." Our aim is not to castigate evaluators for events beyond their control but to suggest that the disappearing act should not come as a surprise. The initial subject population is reduced by, among other things, eligibility requirements, participation rates, treatment completion rates, and posttreatment followup location rates. Thus, the number of subjects the evaluator ends up with will be only some fraction of the initial subject population. The evaluator needs to estimate how many subjects that fraction consists of, whether the number is sufficient, and what implications various strategies for attaining that number have for the research.

There are clear advantages to selecting sites with large client populations for study. In such cases, an adequate sample can be achieved without the additional cost and headaches of multi-site studies. If the level of funding limits the number of data collectors, conducting research at a single site may be the only option. And if the site is not particularly large, one needs to anticipate a long enough data collection period to achieve the required number of subjects.

NDATUS described clinic size from a number of perspectives, including the number of individuals who could be treated on a given day (in terms of beds or maximum average caseload) as well as the number of new individuals over time. The majority of clinics were small: 60 percent had a capacity of twenty-five or fewer clients. This suggested that it might be more difficult to find large clinics than smaller ones. Also, evidence about implementation and effects from atypically large sites may be less generalizable than similar evidence from smaller, more typical ones. Further, since the smaller clinics were more likely to provide short-term treatment, they tended to have a higher dynamic capacity than the large clinics.

Completion rate and average length of stay are other important pieces of information for planning purposes. In the area of drug abuse treatment, both methadone maintenance and long-term RDF treatment, clients complete at a relatively low rate (10 to 20 percent of admissions) and after relatively long treatment stays (one to two years). These data have implications for the duration and cost of a longitudinal outcome study: How long will the study have to run to accumulate sufficient numbers of graduates?

Estimating the feasibility of the plan also requires a good working knowledge of clinic procedures. Thus, while it may be desirable to match subjects on dosage level, one needs to know the number of clients taking around the same dose to estimate whether it is possible to do so. Also, how clients move through the treatment system may have implications for the plan. Consider an evaluation that includes training clinical staff to provide an experimental treatment. If clients typically move from one unit to another within the system, disrupting continuity of the experimental treatment or requiring that a great number of staff will have to receive special training, the evaluation may not be feasible.

*Identifying Likely Interactions.* Interactions refer to differences in the effectiveness of treatment at different levels of a variable. With reference to our program framework, we suggest that treatment variables can interact with other treatment variables as well as with organizational, client, and environmental factors. For example, the effectiveness of a particular form of treatment can vary at different levels of treatment intensity (treatment by treatment interaction), staff training (treatment by administering organization), client motivation (treatment by client audience), funding (treatment by political/regulatory context), and median income in the catchment area (treatment by community context). Information about interactions is useful for a variety of reasons. If a program is, on average, effective, it may be possible to increase its impact by identifying client subgroups it could be treating or by streamlining procedures and focusing on the active ingredients of the treatment process. If a program is, on average, ineffective, it may still be possible that it works quite well for certain types of clients or in certain settings.

The possible number of interactions is enormous. Chen and Rossi (1984) write, "any treatment as delivered can be broken down analytically into a very large number of identifiable components, the vast majority of which may have trivial impacts upon outcomes. Identifying the important components is again the task of applying a priori knowledge and theory" (p. 348). Light (1984) illustrates how research synthesis can identify interactions.

Program information provides another perspective on interactions. One may generate hypotheses about interactions by examining how different procedures are used with particular clients across settings. The actual pattern of procedures and clients in different settings may indicate a problem that the program may be able to fix, a potential confound that the evaluator needs to control for, or clinical wisdom regarding optimal use of program resources that warrants further study.

The pattern that emerged from the RDF preassessment suggested that short-term clinics were primarily alcoholism treatment units. Almost two-thirds of short-term clinics reported that the primary drug of abuse for the majority of their clients was alcohol, compared to 10 percent of long-term clinics. Also, 71 percent of total funding for short-term clinics was allocated for alcoholism treatment, compared to 36 percent of total funding for long-term programs. Short-term clinics served older patients (more than a third of clients in short-term clinics were thirty or older, compared to 13 percent in long-term clinics), who were more likely to be employed and married than residents in long-term clinics. Short-term clinics tended to be smaller (median capacity eighteen compared to thirty-three for long-term), more likely to be funded by private health insurance (31 percent compared to 10 percent) and to have a higher cost per client (median per-day cost $38 for short-term and $25 for long-term clinics).

The scope of treatment—that is, the range of problems addressed—was narrower in short-term than in the long-term clinics, and fewer mediators were posted. Resource variables interacted with client variables in influencing the selection process. Clients with insurance entered hospital-based, short-term projects despite the nature and severity of behavioral problems, whereas clients without insurance tended to end up in longer-term projects. Examining how these variables relate to one another, one may hypothesize that varying levels of treatment intensity are being matched to subgroups with varying levels of need. The variability among projects permits tests of the hypothesized differential effectiveness of short- and long-term treatment with different types of clients, with the possibility of increasing the effectiveness of the matching process.

*Anticipating Unintended Effects.* Morash (1984) describes social impact assessment, a procedure for anticipating a broad range of program impacts prior to replicating a treatment. The goal of the process is to provide planners, administrators, and other interested individuals with information about unintended as well as intended impacts on third parties as well as on the target group. The process can be used to identify how the treatment may need to be modified to fit the constraints of the setting. In a less formal way, our survey of drug-abuse treatment clinics pointed to potential problems inherent in a shift toward short-term treatment. Two examples will illustrate the nature of these potential problems.

Staff morale was low in some clinics where planned treatment duration had been reduced. Staff complained that they were expected to accomplish as much as before in less time. They expressed frustration at not being able to deal with the range or depth of clients' problems that they felt needed to be addressed. In those clinics where staff morale was not a problem, administrative and counseling staff had spent time talking about what the shorter treatment duration meant with respect to planned outcomes and had attempted to redefine the nature and scope of the content of treatment. It appears that, when planned treatment duration is reduced arbitrarily, staff commitment to the treatment process may erode. When staff were given the opportunity to reevaluate the treatment theory, receive additional training, and develop an investment in the redesigned treatment, staff commitment remained high.

Furthermore when short-term clinics were compared to the more traditional long-term model, the outline of a two-tiered system became evident. As one respondent put it, the short-term model is for "top-shelf" addicts. These clients tended to be older, socially stable, and have insurance to cover the costs of treatment. Clients in long-term clinics were more likely to be nonwhite, with limited resources, and were typically referred by the criminal justice system. As clinics look increasingly to third-party sources of funding to make up losses in government support, low SES and uninsured persons risk being squeezed out of the system. The task of state and regional planners will be to take advantage of third-party sources of fundung whenever possible to support the treatment system as a whole, and to provide incentives to clinics to maintain a mix of insured and uninsured clients.

*Clues to the Stability of Measures.* Circumstances will change during an evaluation, but careful planning can keep costly mid-course corrections to a minimum. Some elements in an evaluation of a social program do not change; they transmogrify. The survival of social programs requires a certain political agility, which in turn is predicated on keeping objectives and definitions vague. Thus, evaluators who believe they have a good grasp of local realities at the onset of an evaluation may be baffled when these realities subsequently change or disappear.

One way of assessing the stability of a program's terminology is to track program descriptors over time. For example, we selected clinics to survey from the 1979 NDATUS, and then obtained descriptive data on those clinics from the 1980 NDATUS. Thus we had information on individual clinics for two consecutive years. We were not surprised to find that some clinics had closed between 1979 and 1980. We were, however, surprised to find that others had changed their primary orientation. Primary orientation refers to the types of treatment services that the clinic is funded to provide. The categories include drug abuse treatment only, alcoholism treatment only, and combined drug and alcoholism treatment. After noting the a sizeable number of clinics classified as drug treatment units in 1979 were classified as alcoholism treatment units in 1980, we discovered that, under the regulation, clinics with one or more drug abusing clients could be classified as drug abuse treatment clinics. When they lost those (possibly few) clients, they lost their status as a drug abuse clinic.

Another way to evaluate measures is to compare multiple sources of data. As noted, we had two sources of program data, NDATUS and our own survey of clinics. Both surveys asked about the primary treatment orientation of the clinic. According to NDATUS, 60 percent of responding clinics provided only drug abuse treatment while 31 percent provided combined treatment. According to the survey of clinics, 30 percent indicated that they provided only drug abuse treatment while 63 percent provided combined treatment. We ultimately surmised that, since clinics were not funded by NIDA to provide alcoholism treatment, clinics were underreporting this activity to the funding agency.

## Conclusion

This chapter describes several uses of descriptive information about programs in planning evaluations. What conclusions can be drawn about such data? One generalization relates to the relative utility of program data compared to other sources of planning information, such as study- and site-specific data. A second relates to the adequacy with which national data bases such as NDATUS describe programs.

In planning evaluations, program information contributes to a middle ground between what Cordray and Sonnefeld (this volume) label as macro-level planning decisions and micro-level planning decisions. Program information is distinct from the methodological considerations leading to choices among designs (macro-level) and from the site-specific constraints leading to decisions about operational elements of the design (micro-level); but program information may serve to inform both classes of decisions. With respect to macro-level decisions, program information may help the researchers estimate the relevance of the evaluation's objectives. Information about the conditions under which the program operates suggests questions to be addressed which are program-related and thus likely to be of interest to program managers. Design and method decisions, in turn, are contingent upon the questions selected for study.

With respect to micro-level decisions, program information may help the evaluator estimate the reasonableness of the evaluation plan. Once the issues have been decided and before proceding to a consideration of site-specific data, the evaluator may wish to consider whether the plan is feasible, given what is already known about the program. Thus, if the average cost of providing treatment is low, how likely is it that costs can be further reduced? When the evaluator does consider site-specific data in order to decide, for example, how long the evaluation will have to run, contrasting these data with summary information across sites tells the evaluator how representative eligible sites will be. Or, a large discrepancy between the program norms and characteristics of the site may alert the evaluator to construct or measurement problems. For example, if the average length of stay (LOS) across sites is three months and the clinic claims an average LOS of twelve, they may be calculating LOS for a subset of admissions, or including aftercare in their calculations, and so on. When site-specific data are unavailable, the normative data can serve as expected values.

How adequately does a monitoring data base describe a program? The major strength of a national monitoring data base such as NDATUS is its coverage. NDATUS attempted to collect information from all known drug abuse and alcoholism clinics in the United States, regardless of sources of funding. In 1982, 3,018 drug abuse facilities responded to NDATUS (National Institute on Drug Abuse, 1983). NDATUS attempted to ensure high quality data by holding national training conferences, providing technical assistance to the states, distributing data collection manuals, and enlisting the cooperation of states in identifying clinics and in editing the completed data forms.

The major weakness is its limited scope. If we compare the scope of NDATUS to the program model illustrated in Figure 1, we find that

NDATUS focuses on the implementation system and provides little information about treatment per se or the environmental context. Some trade-off between coverage and scope is inevitable. The cost alone of obtaining detailed treatment, implementation, and contextual information about several thousand clinics would be prohibitive, even if one could imagine a use for such data.

The implementation data are considered essential by the monitoring agency to determine whether general legislative aims are being met, funds are being spent appropriately, and targeted clients are being served by the program. Evaluations, we are frequently told, do not provide program managers with the service delivery information they need. A system such as NDATUS, designed and used by program managers, is a useful guide to the data elements program managers consider important. As the field of program evaluation becomes increasingly sensitive to the need to characterize the program in evaluation reports, monitoring systems can serve as a checklist of possible implementation variables.

At the same time, program monitoring data are inadequate for researchers' needs. In addition to the lack of treatment data, NDATUS lacks a theoretical perspective that would identify important variables and suggest relationships among them. The researcher would have the monitoring agency resolve the tradeoff between sample size and amount of information per site differently, by collecting more comprehensive information from fewer sites.

In summary, national program data can be a useful tool in the evaluation planning process. Such data can alert evaluators to program managers' perceived needs and provide an overview of local realities. While the data may be limited in scope and devoid of theoretical considerations, these data should also be more representative than study- or site-specific data. Such data bases, limited as they are, contain the most comprehensive descriptions of program contexts currently available. The field of evaluation is challenged to improve upon these program models.

## References

Chen H.-T., and Rossi, P. H. "Evaluating with Sense: The Theory-Driven Approach." In R. F. Conner, D. G. Altman, and C. Jackson (Eds.), *Evaluation Studies Review Annual.* (Vol. 9). Beverly Hills, Calif.: Sage Publications, 1984.

Cook, T. D. "Opportunities for Evaluation in the Next Few Years." In R. F. Conner, D. G. Altman, and C. Jackson (Eds.), *Evaluation Studies Review Annual.* (Vol. 9). Beverly Hills, Calif.: Sage Publications, 1984.

Cronbach, L. J., and Associates. *Toward Reform of Program Evaluation: Aims, Methods, and Institutional Arrangements.* San Francisco, Calif.: Jossey-Bass, 1980.

Devine, E., O'Connor, F., and Wenk, V. Personal communication, January 1985.

Dole, V. P., and Nyswander, M. E. "Methadone Maintenance Treatment: A Ten-Year Perspective." *Journal of the American Medical Association,* 1976, *235,* 2117–2119.

Hendricks, M. "Service Delivery Assessment: Qualitative Evaluations at the Cabinet Level." In E. R. House, S. Mathison, J. A. Pearsol, and H. Preskill (Eds.), *Evaluation Studies Review Annual.* (Vol.7). Beverly Hills, Calif.: Sage Publications, 1982.

Holland, S. "Evaluating Community-based Treatment Programs: A Model for Strengthening Inferences About Effectiveness." *International Journal of Therapeutic Communities,* 1983, *4,* 285–306.

Light, R. J. "Six Evaluation Issues that Synthesis Can Resolve Better Than Individual Studies." In W. H. Yeaton and P. M. Wortman (Eds.), *Issues in Data Synthesis.* New Directions for Program Evaluation, no. 24. San Francisco, Calif.: Jossey-Bass, 1984.

Love, A. J. "The Organizational Context and the Development of Internal Evaluation." In A. J. Love (Ed.), *Developing Effective Internal Evaluation.* New Directions for Program Evaluation, no. 20. San Francisco, Calif.: Jossey-Bass, 1983.

Lukoff, I. F. "Issues in the Evaluation of Heroin Treatment." In E. Josephson and E. E. Carroll (Eds.), *Drug Use: Epidemiological and Sociological Approaches.* New York, N.Y.: Hemisphere, 1974.

Moos, R. H., and Finney, J. W. "The Expanding Scope of Alcoholism Treatment Evaluation." *American Psychologist,* 1983, *38* (10), 1036–1044.

Morash, M. "The Application of Social Impact Assessment to the Study of Criminal and Juvenile Justice Programs: A Case Study." In R. F. Conner, D. G. Altman, and C. Jackson (Eds.), *Evaluation Studies Review Annual.* (Vol. 9). Beverly Hills, Calif.: Sage Publications, 1984.

National Institute on Drug Abuse. *Main Findings for Drug Abuse Treatment Units, September 1982.* (NIDA Statistical Series F, no. 10, DHHS Publication no. [ADM] 83-1284.) Rockville, Md: National Institute on Drug Abuse, 1983.

Sechrest, L., and Redner, R. *How Well Does it Work? Review of Criminal Justice Evaluation, 1978.* Washington, D.C.: National Institute of Law Enforcement and Criminal Justice, 1979.

Sells, S. B. *Rationale of the Joint NIMH-TCU Drug Abuse Reporting Program.* (IBR Report.) Fort Worth, Tex.: Institute of Behavioral Research, Texas Christian University, 1972.

Simpson, D. D. "Treatment for Drug Abuse: Follow-Up Outcomes and Length of Time Spent." *Archives of General Psychiatry,* 1981, *38,* 875–880.

St. Pierre, R. G., and Cook, T. D. "Sampling Strategy in the Design of Program Evaluation." In R. F. Conner, D. G. Altman, and C. Jackson (Eds.), *Evaluation Studies Review Annual.* (Vol. 9). Beverly Hills, Calif.: Sage Publications, 1984.

*Sherry Holland is director of research for Gateway Foundation, Inc., a substance abuse treatment program in Illinois. Her current research interests include quasi-experimental methodology and the integration of qualitative and quantitative data to inform the decision-making process.*

*The manner in which results and methods are reported influences the utility of the synthesis of prior studies for planning new evaluations. Confidence ratings, coding conventions, and supplemental evidence can partially overcome the difficulties. Planners must acknowledge the influence of their own judgment in using prior research.*

# Obstacles to Using Prior Research and Evaluations

*Robert G. Orwin*

On first impression, improving evaluations by using prior research is a simple, two-stage input-output process. In the first stage, the prior research is the input $(x)$, the evaluator's knowledge yield is the output $(y)$, and $y=f(x)$. In the second stage, the evaluator's knowledge yield is the input, and the improved evaluation plan is the output $(z)$; that is, $z=f(y)$.

Like many first impressions, this one is misleading; the true relationships are considerably more complex. For knowledge yield $(y)$ is not only a function of the research $(x)$, but also of the accuracy, completeness, and clarity with which that research is reported $(r)$. It is also a function of the ability of the evaluator to correctly judge what the reported information signifies about the study $(j)$. When multiple prior studies are used, and the evaluator's intent is to synthesize their results, then the synthesis process itself introduces errors, biases, conceptual slippages, and so on $(e)$. If that were not enough, our new function, $y=f(x,r,j,e)$, will include unspecifiable interactions that may never be adequately understood. The focus of this chapter is the first stage, specifically, the problems that reporting deficiencies and judgment calls pose for systematic research synthesis, that is, meta-analysis.

D. S. Cordray (Ed.). *Utilizing Prior Research in Evaluation Planning.* New Directions for Program Evaluation, no. 27. San Francisco: Jossey-Bass, September 1985.

Reporting Quality

We have identified three sources of deficient reporting: quality of publicizing, quality of macro-level reporting, and quality of micro-level reporting. The effects of these on the synthesis process are illustrated in Figure 1.

*Quality of Publicizing.* The existence of data is often inadequately publicized (for instance, when studies are not written up, lost, or suppressed). This "file drawer problem" (Rosenthal, 1979) can cause sampling bias. Some research synthesis sample unpublished as well as published studies; this reduces the problem but does not eliminate it. To assess the severity of the file drawer threat, the analyst can calculate the "fail safe", $N$, which estimates the number of hypothetical no-effect studies required to bring a significant overall $p$-level up to nonsignificance (Orwin, 1983a; Rosenthal, 1979). Even when the file drawer problem is unlikely to threaten overall findings (for instance, average effect size), subtler and more specific conclusions may still warrant concern, particularly when deduced from a relatively small subset of studies.

*Quality of Macro-Level Reporting.* For studies that are accessible, we have conceptualized reporting quality in two ways: macro-level and micro-level. Macro-level reporting quality refers to the customary reporting practices of the research area being synthesized, and has a two-stage impact. First, it influences the selection of variables for coding by excluding potentially important variables for which information is never, or rarely, reported. Second, it restricts the operationalization of variables that are customarily examined to the measurement options conventional in the research area. This often results in a lack of precision with which a given variable can be mapped.

Through these influences, macro-level reporting quality affects later analyses in predictable ways. Omitting variables that cause effect size variation results in underspecification of statistical models and, consequently, biased parameter estimates for included variables correlated with one or more omitted variables (Campbell and Boruch, 1975). Collapsing continuous variables into gross categorizations can diminish analytic sensitivity and bias parameter estimates (Cohen and Cohen, 1975; Kerlinger and Pedhazur, 1973). More sophisticated analytic strategies (see Hedges, 1982) potentially offer improvements. Structural equation models, for example, can handle both specification error and measurement error in ways that regression/ANCOVA models cannot (Kenney, 1979). The adoption of more sophisticated analysis strategies by synthesists is a welcome development, but will not obviate the need for reporting quality concerns; rather, it will compel more explicit treatment of those concerns.

*Quality of Micro-Level Reporting.* Whereas macro-level reporting quality describes the customary reporting practices of an area, micro-level reporting quality describes the individual differences among the area's investigators

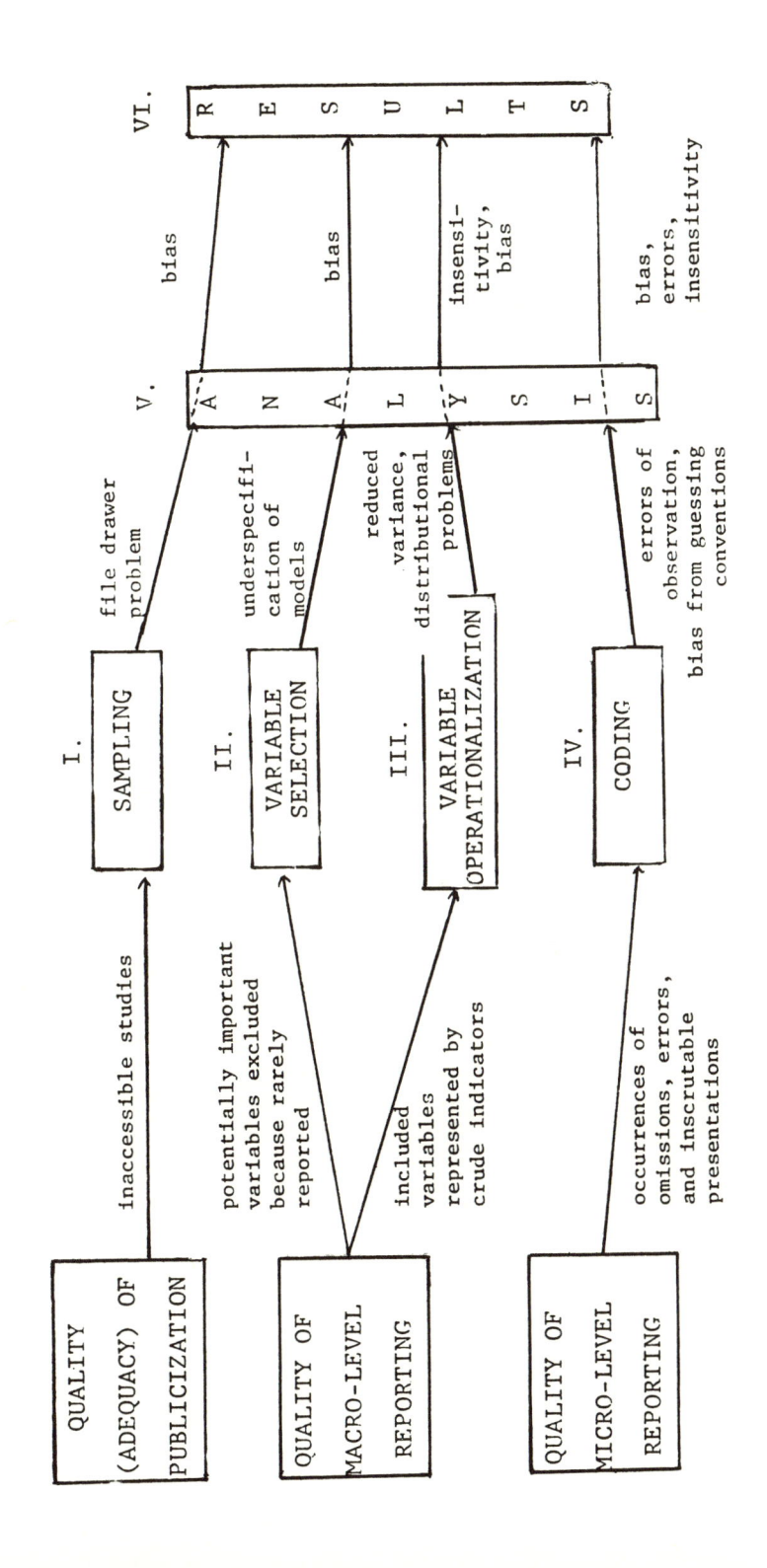

Figure 1. A Model of the Influence of Reporting Quality on Meta-Analytic Results

(that is, report writers) in the completeness, accuracy, and clarity with which those customs are upheld. It influences research synthesis at the coding stage. Inadequate reporting of study characteristics leads to coder uncertainty, which in turn leads to coder error. Recognizing this problem, synthesists sometimes devise coding conventions as a partial solution. When an investigator failed to report therapist experience, for example, Smith and others (1980) assigned experience on the basis of education. Such devices serve to standardize coder decisions under uncertainty and therefore increase intercoder agreement. It is arguable whether they eliminate error, however, since the convention dictated choice will often be wrong.

Micro-level reporting quality, like macro-level, affects later analysis in predictable ways. In the dependent variable, errors of observation destabilize parameter estimates and decrease statistical power, whereas in independent variables, they cause parameter estimates to be biased (Kerlinger and Pedhazur, 1973). Once again, more sophisticated analytical strategies than are presently typical should bring progress, particularly those that allow user-defined measurement models.

*An Empirical Investigation of the Influence of Reporting Quality.* We used the Smith and others (1980) data to assess the influence of reporting quality in quantitative research synthesis (for a more complete description see Orwin, 1983b, or Orwin and Cordray, 1985). In so doing, we identified two sources of information pertinent to investigating the influence of reporting quality: interrater reliabilities and confidence judgments.

*Interrater Reliabilities.* One consequence of differences in micro-level reporting quality—coder error—may be estimated by interrater reliability. Reliability of coding is a concern in research synthesis, and it is common for synthesists to present overall agreement rates as evidence that their coding scheme is reliable (Stock and others, 1982). For example, Smith and others (1980) computed a 92 percent overall agreement rate across a sample of variables over a sample of reports.

There are at least two problems with this practice. First, the coding form is not a multi-item measure of a trait (such that a total scale reliability would be meaningful) but a list of disparate items. Using Smith and others' coding scheme, we had little difficulty replicating their overall agreement rate (ours was .90). However, agreement rates for individual items ranged from .39 to 1.00. Not surprisingly, agreement was near perfect only on simple, universally reported variables (for example, publication date). Consistent with their uncertain meaning, overall agreement rates are difficult to incorporate meaningfully into subsequent analysis; they also fail to identify problematic items needing refinement or replacement.

The second problem is that the use of simple agreement rates as reliability estimates has several pitfalls. When response marginals are extreme, high agreement occurs by chance (Hartmann, 1977). These conditions are commonplace in quantitative research synthesis. Additional problems arise when marginal response rates differ across raters (Cohen, 1960) or when items are ordinal rather than nominal. Finally, it is unclear how to derive a composite agreement rate for more than two raters.

For these reasons we do not recommend the use of agreement rates (overall or item-specific) to demonstrate coding reliability, nor do we recommend their use as proxies for reporting quality. In our reanalysis, we computed several measures of interrater reliability for each coding item and then recalculated all of Smith and others' regression analyses, using our reliability data to correct for attenuation. In the spirit of bracketing effects (Boruch and others, 1981), we recomputed the regression coefficients four times, each time using a different set of reliability estimates. The first run used the highest estimates available for each variable; its purpose was to provide a conservative lower boundary on the amount of change produced by disattenuation. The second, third, and fourth runs were progressively more liberal.

The reliability corrections frequently caused the sign of a predictor's coefficient from the uncorrected run to reverse. The implication of a sign reversal (when significant) is that interpretation of the uncorrected coefficient would have led to an incorrect conclusion regarding the direction of the predictor's influence on effect size. In every run in every class and subclass, the reliability correction altered the ranking of the predictors in their capacity to uniquely account for variance in effect size. Predictors showing promise in the uncorrected run often proved spurious when corrections were put in place; conversely, others were unremarkable in the uncorrected runs but relatively impressive in corrected runs. Smith and others' internal validity variable is a case in point. In all classes and all but one subclass, its ranking relative to the other predictors of effect size increased from the zero run to the fourth run, sometimes dramatically. (In contrast, Smith and others found a correlation of only .03 between internal validity and effect size, which they took as evidence that design quality had no effect.)

*Confidence Ratings.* Reliability alone is a flawed indicator of reporting quality. It stems from coder disagreement which in turn is indicative of coder uncertainty and, through coder uncertainty, deficient reporting. However, good reporting does not guarantee agreement, as coding errors, idiosyncratic interpretations, and judgment calls will sometimes preclude it. Conversely, agreement will sometimes occur when reporting quality is low, either by chance or by predetermined coding conventions. (Statistics like Cohen's K lessen only the chance problem.)

It is therefore desirable to seek more direct methods of identifying well reported information. The use of confidence ratings is based on the premise that questionable information should not be discarded, nor should it be allowed to freely mingle with less questionable information, as is usually done. The former wastes information which, though flawed, may be the best available on a given variable, while the latter injects noise at best and bias at worst into a system already beset by both problems. With confidence ratings, questionable information can be described as such, and both data point and confidence descriptor entered into the data file.

Our confidence scale had three levels: high, medium, and low. As with interrater reliability, we found considerable variation in mean confidence across the coding items from Smith and others (1980). The percentage of high ratings ranged from 9 percent for therapist experience to 100 percent for location of treatment. Note that neither of these variables would be difficult to code were the necessary description information provided; the difference reflects a large difference in micro-level reporting quality. On a per study basis, the percentage of items coded with high confidence ranged from 52 percent to 83 percent. At the opposite end the percentage rated low ranged from 25 percent to 0 percent.

Not surprisingly, confidence was a strong predictor of coder agreement. For example, the mean agreement rate for high confidence items more than doubled that for low confidence items (.92 versus .44). Finally, absolute values of bivariate correlations were considerably larger for high confidence cases than for all cases taken together, reflecting the degradatory effect of deficient reporting quality on observed substantive relationships. Between 71 percent and 82 percent of all bivariate correlations increased, depending on which coder's data was tested, and the sizes of the increases were nontrivial, with means ranging from 63 percent to 77 percent. Correlations with effect size were particularly likely to increase; these were of special importance because the relationships between study characteristics and effect size are a major focus in most research syntheses.

*Summary.* Our reanalysis confirmed the expected effects of both macro-level and micro-level reporting deficiencies, as assessed with interrater reliabilities and confidence ratings. Reliabilities varied greatly across individual coding items, and, when used to correct regression analysis for attenuation, shifted the relative importance of predictors and increased R-squares notably. Confidence ratings varied greatly across both items and studies and were consistently and strongly associated with both reliabilities and the strength of observed relationships between variables. As a whole, the results suggest that deficient reporting injects considerable noise into synthesis data, which can lead to spurious conclusions regarding causes of effect size, adequacy of models, and related matters.

*Coping with Deficient Reporting: What Can Be Done?* Our analysis provided an empirical demonstration of some degradatory effects of deficient reporting and suggested some relatively low-cost procedures to attenuate these. But we do not claim to have solved the problem. The only fully satisfactory solution would be the improvement of reporting itself.

Pious exhortations to primary researchers are not likely to succeed in improving reporting for several reasons. First, there are systematic impediments to writing detailed reports. In articles prepared for scholarly journals, the impediment takes the form to competition for scarce space. The norm is not only to keep articles short, but to let outsiders (editors, referees) largely determine what stays or comes out. In reports prepared within the government, the impediments are different; the competition is not for space but for the attention of higher echelon bureaucrats. In this environment, a brief report is often considered desirable because brevity facilitates wider readership and consequently greater visibility for the report's contents and its authors (Moran, 1982).

Second, primary researchers have no immediate incentive to facilitate a future synthesis that includes their work, even though the ultimate advancement of their area may depend on it. This is analogous to the familiar tragedy of the commons parable used by political scientists (see Ophuls, 1977) to describe situations in which the continued existence of a public good, such as plentiful natural resources, relies on private restraint, such as individual conservation. The present context is further complicated because the commons is still only an abstraction when exploited, and the exploiter (primary researcher) may just as easily consider the synthesis a public nuisance as a public good (a superficial and wholly inappropriate use of the work).

Finally, there are the more blatantly self-serving reasons for omitting or obfuscating selected information in reports. While the prevalence of outright fraud is debatable (Fisher, 1982), the temptation to omit or reconstruct events or other facts that would weaken findings or embarrass the authors is ever present, and it would be naive to assume it was not yielded to with some regularity.

The gatekeepers of social research are in a better position politically to effect change. These powerful influences would be journal editors for scholarly articles, peer review committees for government grant and contract products, and high level agency personnel for internally generated government reports. Lobbying these groups would be more successful than exhorting primary researchers, though how this should be accomplished is unclear.

In the meantime there are at least three ways in which synthesists can counter deficient reporting. First, coder reliability can be taken more seriously than in the past. As demonstrated earlier, separate reliability coefficients for individual coding items, based on appropriate estimators, are much more informative and useful than the commonly used overall agreement rate.

Second, synthesists can rate data quality and incorporate data quality information into analyses. In our study, a three-point confidence scale proved to be a simple, fast, yet effective way to discern well-reported from less well-reported information during subsequent analyses. Alternative indicators and more involved strategies are of course possible.

Third, research synthesists can consider alternate sources of information. Some have attempted to obtain additional information on primary studies by going outside the reports. We are aware of two strategies: contacting the original investigators and exploiting external information sources.

An example of the first strategy is Hyde (1981). Rather than estimating approximate effect sizes from incomplete information, Hyde wrote the authors. Of fifty-three studies, eighteen (34 percent) lacked means and standard deviations. Although all eighteen authors were located and contacted, unfortunately only two were both willing and able to supply the needed information. An example of the second strategy can be found in Smith and others (1980). When the experimenter's affiliation was not evident from the primary report, Smith and others consulted the American Psychological Association directory. Both these strategies are necessarily limited, the first because the odds of success will typically be low, the second because the proportion of variables that are potentially retrievable from external sources will typically be small. Still, synthesists might keep them in mind since instances will surely arise in which their use is warranted.

Another source of information, if obtainable, is the raw microdata from primary studies. The use of microdata is a potentially powerful addition that to date has been underexploited (see Cordray and Orwin, 1983). Its particular relevance to reporting quality is self-evident. Light and Smith (1971) have focused on the integration of microdata to resolve apparent contradictions among studies. Their approach has received high marks from writers on research synthesis but has been little used in practice.

## Judgment Calls

There is some relationship between reporting quality and the need for judgment calls. Deficient reporting of study characteristics increases the need for judgment in coding; this is what our confidence ratings were designed to cope with. Many other variables, however, intrinsically require judgment regardless of reporting quality. In fact, more judgment can be necessary when reporting is thorough, because the coder has more information to weigh.

*Macro-Level Calls.* Again, the macro-level/micro-level distinction will be useful. Macro-level judgments are those that set policy and, in so doing, reflect the overall intents and purposes of the synthesist, including the synthesist's methodological perspective. Several of these have been discussed by Light (1980), who noted that even when a systematic and rigorous statistical procedure is used, judgmental decisions must be made. Light discussed three judgment calls the synthesist must make: (1) which studies should be included, (2) when measures of central tendency are useful as summary statistics, and (3) whether studies control for background variables in similar enough ways to be analyzed together. Although various solutions have been proposed, these questions remain unresolved, and, in fact, may never be resolved.

Compare, for example, two views on the first judgment call raised by Light—selecting which studies to include. Glass (Glass and others, 1981) argues against the a priori exclusion of studies judged methodologically flawed by the synthesist, whereas several of his critics (Eysenck, 1978; Fiske, 1978) argue for it, albeit not necessarily for the same reasons. The issues in this controversy are complex and not easily amenable to empirical resolution. The prospective synthesist must weigh the pros and cons of each position and choose, in other words, make a judgment call.

Some effects of macro-level judgments on findings are directly analogous to the effects of macro-level reporting deficiencies. Omitting variables that cause effect size but are too complex to code has the same potential effects as omitting them because they are poorly reported. Collapsing continuous variables into categorical ones because judgment has limited resolution has the same potential effects as doing so because of reporting deficiencies. Depending on how divergent synthesists' overall approaches are, these effects may be only the tip of the iceberg. In the extreme case, two syntheses which nominally covered the same research literature may show no other commonalities.

*Micro-Level Calls.* The need for judgment calls does not end when the synthesist sets policy (for instance, including only studies with characteristic $X$). Countless other problems crop up in reading studies, quantifying their characteristics, and measuring their outcomes. These are micro-level judgments which serve the intents and purposes established by the macro-level judgments. In other words, macro-level calls set policy and micro-level calls implement it.

In Smith and others' psychotherapy study, for example, all reported outcome measures from a given report were to be coded unless judged by the coder to be redundant. Additional rules guided these decisions, such as whether to combine the subtest scores of a multifactorial test battery. The rules seemed straightforward. Yet for the twenty-five reports that we sampled for our reanalysis, Smith and others coded eight-one outcome measures, while we coded 159 (Orwin) and 172 (Cordray) using the same decision rules as Smith and others. More clarity in the decision rule might have better guided the judgment process, but whether it could have eliminated judgment is debatable. Once the decision rules are formulated and the appropriate observations identified, still more judgment calls are required to code individual variables. As with reporting quality, the degree of judgment required varies widely across variables.

Theoretically, the need for judgment calls in coding could be eliminated by a coding algorithm which considered every possible contingency, and provided the coder with explicit instructions in the event of each one, singly and in every combination. Smith and others' (1980) algorithm for internal validity suggests an attempt at this:

> The internal validity of a study was judged on the basis of the assignment of subjects to treatment and the extent of experimental mortality in the study. To be judged high on the internal validity scale, a study must have used random assignment of subjects to groups and have a rate of mortality less than 15 percent and equivalent between the two groups. If mortality was higher or nonequivalent, internal validity was still rated high if the experimenter included the scores of the terminators in the posttest statistics or established the initial equivalence of terminators and nonterminators. Medium internal validity ratings were given to (1) studies with randomization but high or differential mortality; (2) studies with "failed" randomization procedures (for instance, where the experimenter began by randomizing, but then resorted to other allocation methods, such as taking the last ten clients and putting them into the control group) with low mortality; and (3) extremely well-designed matching studies. Low validity studies were those whose matching procedures were quite weak or nonexistent (for instance, where intact convenience samples were used) or where mortality was severely disproportionate. Occasionally, statistical or measurement irregularities decreased the value assigned to internal validity, such as when an otherwise weak-designed study employed different testing times for treated and untreated groups (pp. 63–64).

The components of this decision rule represent generally accepted internal validity concerns. Yet in trying to apply it, we frequently found that it failed to accommodate some important contingencies and this put our own sense of the study's internal validity in contradiction with the score yielded by the algorithm. For example, in a study on the effects of high school counseling, 870 students from four schools were alternately assigned to the experimental and control groups. This variant of systematic sampling is effectively random, yet not strictly so. In the same study, mortality was virtually identical in the two groups; however it was greater than 15 percent (26 percent, to be precise). The mortality appeared to have been largely caused by students' families moving away from the area high schools. We doubt that family moves were significantly affected by their child's participation in school counseling, particularly since there was no sign of differential attrition. In sum, two reasonable requirements for high internal validity in Smith and others' coding algorithm proved quite unreasonable in this case. But the fault is not with the algorithm's failure to include and instruct on all contingencies, for in practice that would not be possible. In a construct as complex as internal validity, no amount of preliminary work on the coding algorithm will eliminate the need for judgment calls. Indeed, the contingency instructions are judgment calls themselves so, at best, the point of judgment has only been moved, not eliminated.

*An Example: Treatment Integrity.* Numerous variables pose judgment problems for the coder. One such variable is treatment integrity, that is, the extent to which the delivered treatment measures up to the intended treatment. We have selected treatment integrity to exemplify the problem because it routinely will require considerable judgment, and it is of particular relevance to evaluation researchers (Boruch and Gomez, 1977; Sechrest and others, 1979). In the psychotherapy literature synthesized by Smith and others (1980) attrition from treatment (but not from measurement), spotty attendance, failure to meet advertised theoretical requirements, and assorted other implementation problems all potentially degraded treatment integrity. Smith and others did not attempt to code treatment integrity per se, although they did code their degree of confidence that the labels placed on therapies by authors did describe what actually transpired. We attempted to code integrity more globally, with not much success. The following examples point up some of the difficulties:

*Case One* (Shapiro and Knapp, 1971): The efficacy of ego therapy was tested against a placebo treatment and no-treatment controls. Several participants did not attend every session; only those attending four or more sessions out of seven were posttested.

*Case Two* (Marshall and others, 1976): The comparative efficacy of therapist-administered desensitization and self-administered desensitization was tested (relative to various control groups) for reducing public speaking anxiety. The therapists were advanced graduate students in clinical psychology who had been trained in the use of desensitization, but were inexperienced in its application.

*Case Three* (Hogan and Kirchner, 1968): The comparative efficacy of implosive therapy, eclectic verbal therapy, and bibliotherapy was tested for reducing fear of snakes. All eclectic verbal therapy was performed by the second author, who had previously published several articles on implosive therapy.

Case One exemplifies by far the most common treatment integrity problem we encountered: the potential dilution of the treatment regimen by nonattendance. Here the coder must judge whether participants with absentee rates up to 43 percent can be said to have received the intended treatment. If not, by how much was it degraded, and how did this degradation affect the estimated effect size (a question made still more difficult by the authors' failure to report the number of participants with nonattendance problems). In Case Two, the treatment as advertised is potentially degraded by the use of inexperienced treatment providers. The coder must judge whether the lack of practice made a difference, and if so, by how much. In Case Three, the treatment provider's motivation to maintain the integrity of the treatment comes into question. The coder must judge whether the apparent conflict of interest degraded the treatment, and if so, by how much (for instance, uninspired compliance or outright sabotage).

*Coping with Judgment Calls: What Can Be Done?* Reporting quality may improve over time, in fact there are indications that it already has been improving significantly, at least in some areas (Orwin, 1983b). By way of contrast, no external fix could eliminate or even reduce the need for judgment calls. Substantive expertise, while not reducing the need for judgment calls, will increase their accuracy. Numerous writers on research synthesis have stressed the need for substantive expertise, and with good reason—the synthesist who possesses it makes more informed and thoughtful judgments at all levels. Still, scholars with comparable expertise disagree frequently on matters of judgment in the social sciences as elsewhere. Substantive expertise informs judgment, but will not guarantee that the right call was made.

There is little advice we can offer at the macro level. To be sure, we have formed opinions on how quantitative synthesis should and should not be performed, but that only says that we have made some macro-level judgment calls, not that we have learned the secret of making them correctly. At the micro level, we recommend something similar to our confidence ratings on reporting quality. In other words, two confidence ratings could be employed, one rating confidence in the accuracy of the information, and the other rating confidence in the coding interpretation applied to that information. In this way, suspect judgments, just as suspect reporting can be isolated at the analysis stage.

## References

Boruch, R. F., Cordray, D. S., and Wortman, P. M. "Secondary Analysis: Why, When, and How." In R. F. Boruch, P. M. Wortman, and D. S. Cordray (Eds.), *Reanalyzing Program Evaluations.* San Francisco, Calif.: Jossey-Bass, 1981.

Boruch, R. F., and Gomez, H. "Sensitivity, Bias, and Theory in Impact Evaluation." *Professional Psychology,* 1977, *8,* 411–434.

Campbell, D. T., and Boruch, R. F. "Making the Case for Randomized Assignment to Treatment by Considering the Alternatives: Six Ways in Which Quasi-Experimental Evaluations Tend to Underestimate Effects. In C. A. Bennett and A. A. Lumsdaine (Eds.), *Evaluation and Experience: A National Debate.* (Vol. 3). *Disadvantaged Child.* New York, N.Y.: Academic Press, 1975.

Cohen, J. "A Coefficient of Agreement for Nominal Scales." *Educational and Psychological Measurement,* 1960, *20,* 37–46.

Cohen, J., and Cohen, P. *Applied Multiple Regression/Correlation Analysis for the Behavioral Sciences.* Hillsdale, N.J.: Lawrence Erlbaum, 1975.

Cordray, D. S., and Orwin, R. G. "Improving the Quality of Evidence: Interconnections Among Primary Evaluation, Secondary Analysis, and Quantitative Synthesis." In R. J. Light (Ed.), *Evaluation Studies Review Annual.* (Vol. 8). Beverly Hills, Calif.: Sage, 1983.

Eysenck, H. J. "An Exercise in Mega-Silliness" [Comment]. *American Psychologist,* 1978, *33,* 517.

Fisher, K. "The Spreading Stain of Fraud." *APA Monitor,* 1982, *13,* 1, 7–8.

Fiske, D. W. "The Several Kinds of Generalization" [Comment]. *The Behavioral and Brain Sciences,* 1978, *1,* 393.

Glass, G. V., McGaw, B., and Smith, M. L. *Meta-Analysis in Social Research.* Beverly Hills, Calif.: Sage, 1981.

Hartmann, D. P. "Considerations in the Choice of Interobserver Reliability Estimates." *Journal of Applied Behavior Analysis,* 1977, *10,* 103–116.

Hedges, L. V. "Fitting Continuous Models to Effect Size Data." *Journal of Educational Statistics,* 1982, *7,* 245–270.

Hogan, R. A., and Kirchner, J. H. "Implosive, Eclectic, Verbal, and Bibliotherapies in the Treatment of Fears of Snakes." *Behavior Research and Therapy,* 1968, *6,* 167–171.

Hyde, J. S. "How Large Are Cognitive Gender Differences? A Meta-Analysis Using $\omega^2$ and D. *American Psychologist,* 1981, 36, 892–901.

Kenney, D. A. *Correlation and Causation.* New York, N.Y.: Wiley, 1979.

Kerlinger, F. N., and Pedhazur, E. J. *Multiple Regression in Behavioral Research.* New York. N.Y.: Holt, Rinehart, 1973.

Light, R. J. "Synthesis Methods: Some Judgment Calls That Must Be Made". *Evaluation in Education,* 1980, *4,* 13–17.

Light, R. J., and Smith, P. V. "Accumulating Evidence: Procedures for Resolving Contradictions Among Different Studies." *Harvard Educational Review,* 1971, *41,* 429–471.

Marshall, W. L., Presse, L., and Andrews, W. R. "A Self-Administered Program for Public Speaking Anxiety." *Behavior Research and Therapy,* 1976, *14,* 33–39.

Moran, W. C. Personal communication, November, 1982. W. H. Freeman, 1977.

Ophuls, W. *Ecology and the Politics of Scarcity.* San Francisco: W. H. Freeman, 1977.

Orwin, R. G. "A Fail-Safe N for Effect Size." *Journal of Educational Statistics,* 1983a, *8,* 157–159.

Orwin, R. G. "The Influence of Reporting Quality in Primary Studies on Meta-Analytic Outcomes; A Conceptual Framework and Reanalysis." Ph.D. Dissertation, Northwestern University, 1983b.

Orwin, R. G., and Cordray, D. S. "The Effects of Deficient Reporting on Meta-Analysis: A Conceptual Framework and Reanalysis." *Psychological Bulletin,* 1985, *97,* (1), 134–147.

Rosenthal, R. "The File Drawer Problem and Tolerance for Null Results." *Psychological Bulletin,* 1979, *86,* 638–641.

Sechrest, L., West, S. G., Phillips, M. A., Redner, R., and Yeaton, W. H. "Some Neglected Problems in Evaluation Research: Strength and Integrity of Treatments." In L. Sechrest, S. G. West, M. A. Phillips, R. Redner, and W. H. Yeaton (Eds.), *Evaluation Studies Review Annual.* (Vol. 4). Beverly Hills, Calif.: Sage, 1979.

Shapiro, S. B., and Knapp, D. M. "The Effect of Ego Therapy on Personality Integration." *Psychotherapy: Theory, Research, and Practice,* 1971, *8,* 208–212.

Smith, M. L. "Sex Bias in Counseling and Psychotherapy." *Psychological Bulletin,* 1980, *87,* 392–407.

Smith, M. L., Glass, G. V., and Miller, T. I. *The Benefits of Psychotherapy.* Baltimore, Md.: Johns Hopkins University Press, 1980.

Stock, W. A., Okun, M. A., Haring, M. J., Miller, W., and Kinney, C. "Rigor in Data Synthesis: A Case Study of Reliability in Meta-Analysis." *Educational Researcher,* 1982, *11,* 10–20.

*Robert G. Orwin is social science analyst in the Program Evaluation and Methodology Division at the U.S. General Accounting Office, Washington D.C. He is currently working on several evaluations of defense programs. (The statements and opinions in this chapter do not represent official U.S. General Accounting Office policy.)*

*Quality control in the auditing profession has developed useful practices that are applicable to the research and evaluation process. By identifying and controlling sources of bias and noise in our system of inquiry, the quality of evaluative evidence can be enhanced for both present and future use.*

# Quality Control in Evaluation

*William M. K. Trochim*
*Ronald J. Visco*

Evaluations are often plagued with high error rates, data losses, inaccurate program information and other quality problems (Trochim, 1981) that lead to serious and legitimate questioning of the interpretability and sensibility of the evaluation results. This situation has become widely recognized over the past few years, especially in the wake of major studies like the Holtzman Report (Boruch and Cordray, 1980); the increased use of secondary analysis (Boruch, Wortman, and Cordray, 1981) and metaevaluation (Glass and others, 1981; Rosenthal, 1984); and, the rise of the General Accounting Office as a Federal Agency frequently responsible for the synthesis of large numbers of separate evaluations and for judgments of their quality (U.S. General Accounting Office, 1982).

  The evaluation profession has attempted to address the quality issue in a number of ways. Clearly, the most obvious way was to point to established methodological writings as the criteria for quality research. Thus, we see the usual frequent citations of Kish (1965), Cook and Campbell (1979), Nunnally (1978), Hays (1973) and many others who explain what constitutes good practice in sampling, measurement, research design, and data analysis. A second approach has arisen more directly from practice—from the needs of evaluators who had to make judgments about the quality of the evaluations they were receiving. An excellent example of this is the work of Crane and her associates (Crane, 1979; Crane and Maye, 1980) who attempt to determine error rates in aggregate data based on random sampling of the individual studies on which the aggregation was based. A more recent approach to the improvement of evaluation quality is reflected: in the development of standards or guidelines for the profession, namely the Standards of the Evaluation Research Society (ERS Standards Committee, 1982) and of the Joint Committee on Standards for Educational Evaluation (1981).

We hope to augment these approaches to improving evaluation quality by discussing several simple, relatively inexpensive quality assurance techniques that can be incorporated into evaluations. These techniques are used in the fields where quality assurance is necessary, namely the fields of auditing, accounting, and industrial quality control. Despite their apparent utility, there has been little attempt to use these techniques in the field of evaluation. We take to heart Tabor's (1978) caveat that "there is no single system of internal control that would be uniformly applicable to any class of social programs," but hold that the translation of the principles discussed here to other evaluation contexts should be easily manageable.

## Auditing and Accounting

Most businesses use standard accounting and auditing practices to manage and guarantee the integrity of their financial information. These procedures have hardly ever been applied to improve the quality of evaluation data. This section describes one major application from each profession that might be useful in evaluation contexts.

### Internal Control

*Description.* In order to ensure quality of research it is necessary to have a clear understanding of what is to be implemented. This includes an overview of the entire research system and a description of lines of responsibility. In industrial and business contexts, the delineation of the accounting system and the assessment of its quality are usually the task of the auditor. A major auditing function involves the determination of the internal control of the system in question (Hermanson, and others, 1976; Arens and Loebbecke, 1980). Typically, the auditor begins by dividing the whole system into subsystems or transaction cycles, which are more distinct and easily studied. These might include the sales function, payroll and personnel, accounts receivable, accounts payable, and so on. Each of these transaction cycles is studied until their processes can be described well. In most cases, a detailed flow chart that shows how individual transactions proceed through the particular subsystem is made. At some point, the auditor must identify critical points on the flow chart and examine whether sufficient controls exist to insure the integrity of the transaction information. An important guiding principle is the division of responsibility. For instance, persons who are in charge of disbursing cash in an organization should not also have sole responsibility for the record keeping of those transactions. Once the subsystem is understood, the auditor attempts to determine where control is breaking down. This involves empirical investigations, often called compliance tests, to see where discrepancies arise between the ideal system and its implementation. Depending on the circumstances, the auditor might examine records at several key points or follow single transactions through all or part of a cycle. The individual transaction cycles are linked and cross-cycle compliance checks are performed. The results of the internal control study are integrated with other information (for instance, the capabilities and quality of staff) into a final report that states whether the auditor believes error is within acceptable limits.

*Application.* Procedures like the one described above are almost never followed to ensure quality of evaluation data even though they are straightforward, economically viable (at least on a small scale), and have obvious advantages. Most evaluation contexts have no formal definitions of data cycles. Few have or could easily develop flow chart descriptions of their research system. Little attention is paid to who is responsible for what tasks, and seldom are check points established for assuring data integrity. Few researchers monitor such matters except in informal, poorly recorded ways.

However, procedures for conducting evaluation internal control studies are simple to envision. One must begin by describing manageable subcycles of the research process that can be studied separately. For instance, many evaluations, especially summative or outcome ones, can be divided along methodological lines into six definable subsystems: 1. *Sampling.* The process of enumerating the population and correctly drawing the sample for the study. 2. *Measurement.* The process of administering any tests, interviews or observational scales. 3. *Design.* The process of implementing the design. In most outcome research. (This primarily involves the process of assignment to program groups.) 4. *Program.* The process of enacting the program or treatment condition (and comparisons, if appropriate). 5. *Data Preparation.* The process of preparing data for analysis, including any data exclusions, additions, aggregation, and index formation. 6. *Analysis.* The process of analyzing the data, either quantitatively or qualitatively. These subsystems offer a general framework for analysis, but should not be applied literally in all cases. For instance, in many small-scale mental health and educational evaluations, sampling from a population is less relevant than accurate measurement. Further, one need not be as concerned about defining the category into which a particular research step falls as about assuring that all important steps are included somewhere.

*Illustration.* To illustrate the flow-charting task in this context, we can examine the system used to conduct Chapter I compensatory education evaluation in the Providence, Rhode Island, School District. Figure 1 shows a gross overview of all the subsystems involved. Sampling issues are minimal˙ (data are generally recorded for entire student populations), but serious implementation questions arise in all of the remaining subsystems. For example, see the overview of the measurement subsystem shown in Figure 2. The subsystem is divided into three major steps: preparation, administration and packaging and correction. Figure 3 provides an example of how each step, test preparation in this case, can be broken down even further. This level of specificity is probably sufficient for internal control in educational research. Each box on the chart refers to some checkpoint question that could be examined to determine system integrity. A first step in determining control, using this chart would be to identify the person or persons responsible for each question. For example, the question "Were correct materials received?" requires a clerk to check this in the central evaluation office. The question "Were materials correctly distributed to schools?" is the joint responsibility of the schools and the central evaluation office and so on.

The principle of segregation of responsibility implies the types of controls that might be useful at various points. For instance, if one person is responsible for one or more steps in a sequence, it might be appropriate to have another individual, preferably from another department, sign off on the work. When multiple responsible agents are assigned to a single task, one can look for possibilities for redundant record keeping (or double bookkeeping as described below). In many educational settings, a good first step towards quality would involve the clear delineation of responsibility and the construction of sign-off points at key places of the flow chart. This would force the evaluator to be clearer about the specific criteria for acceptability and would increase the awareness and public accountability of the responsible agents. Once the system is understood, one can begin to check its compliance with these criteria of quality. At some points in the measurement subsystem, for example, it would be efficacious to select a sample of tests or classrooms to check quality.

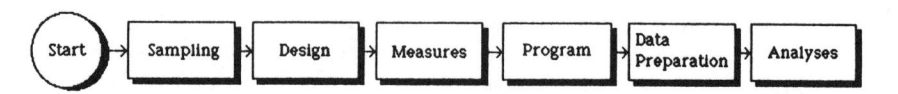

Figure 1. Overview of Possible Subsystems in an Internal Control Study in an Educational Evaluation Context.

Start → Sampling → Design → Measures → Program → Data Preparation → Analyses

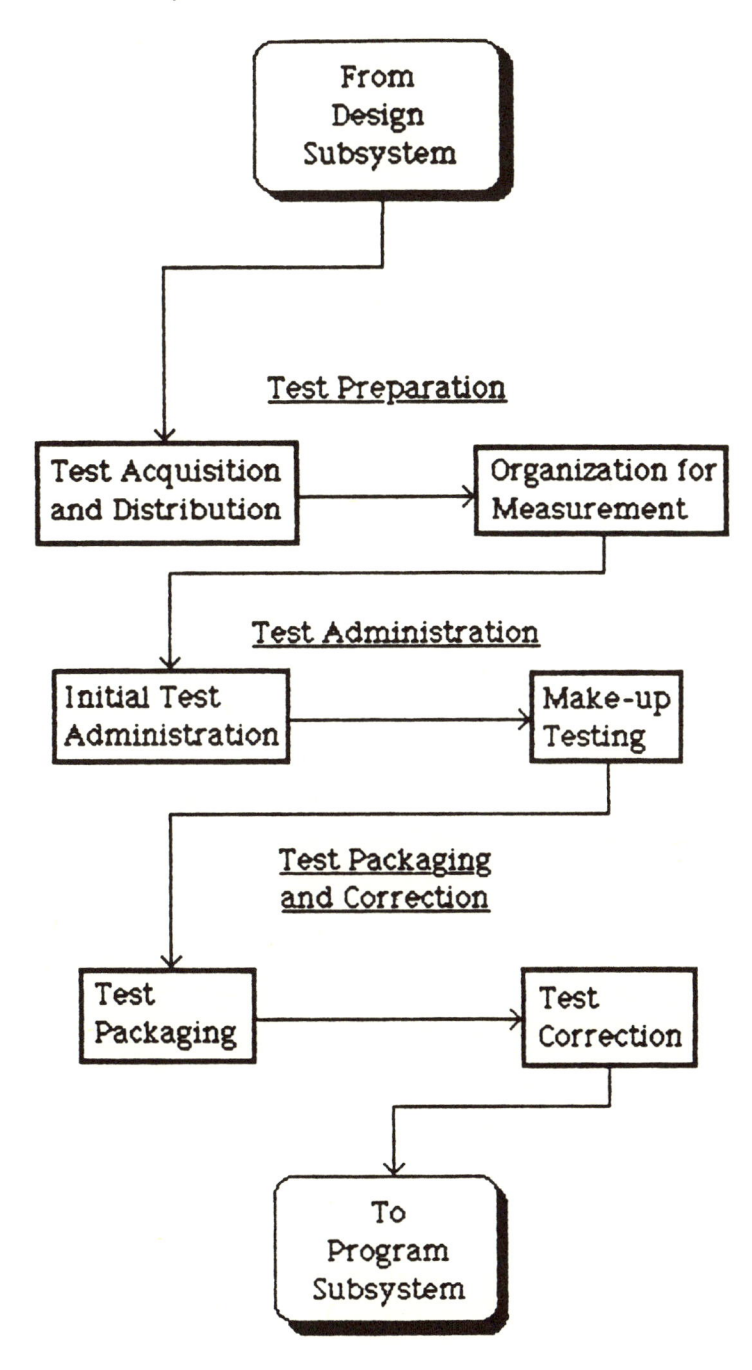

Figure 2. A Sample Measurement Subsystem in an Internal Control Study in an Educational Evaluation Context.

Figure 3. A Sample Measurement Subsystem in an Internal Control Study in an Educational Evaluation Study (Detailed view, Part 1).

## **Test Preparation**

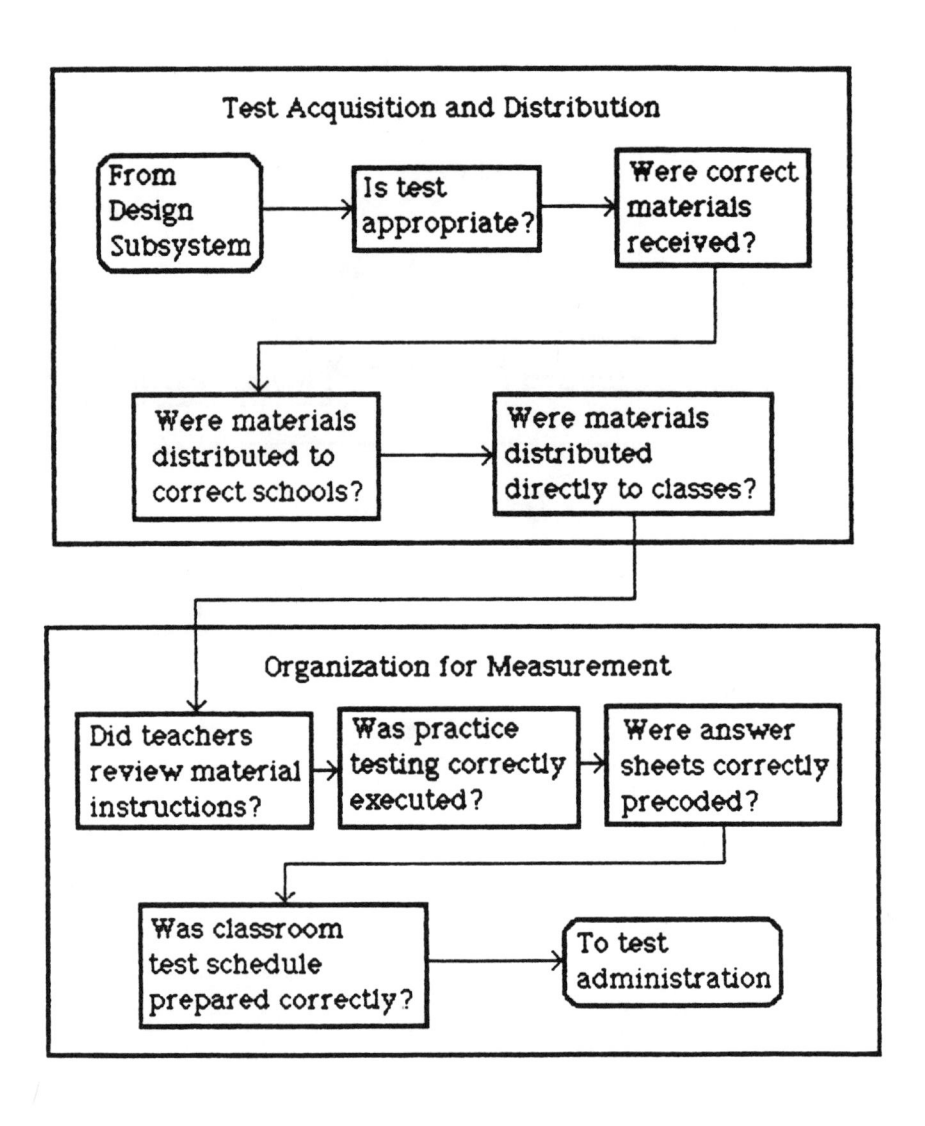

*Double Bookkeeping*

*Description.* The accounting profession is devoted to assuring the accuracy of financial information and utilizes strategies that could be helpful for improving research quality. Tabor (1978) provides an excellent discussion on evaluation data corruption from an accounting perspective. One major accounting procedure—double bookkeeping—has considerable potential for improving the quality of research.

Double bookkeeping strategies are probably the single most important methodological tool in the accounting profession. It involves keeping two independent records of each financial transaction. Each ledger is labelled "credit and debit" and "income and expenses." The built-in redundancy of double bookkeeping guarantees that there will be some independent information to ensure the accuracy of the data.

*Application.* Double bookkeeping procedures can be applied to one of the most difficult problems in many program evaluations—determining who received the program or treatment and for how long. In educational settings, for instance, students are added to or dropped from programs throughout the school year even when the dictates of good evaluation indicate that it is not advantageous to do so. Also, most school districts have standard procedures for challenging students to move into or out of the Chapter I program on the basis of teacher, parent, or administrator views that the child was incorrectly assigned. The possibility of losing track of which students are receiving the program is great, especially if record keeping is poor. Usually districts take a census at some regular interval and this acts as a snapshot view of school membership, though its day-to-day accuracy is questionable. A double bookkeeping system could improve ongoing record keeping between censuses.

Double bookkeeping also has value in settings where individual program participants cycle in and out of the institution. This is often the case in health or mental health evaluations where the clients begin or end treatment as needed rather than on a predetermined schedule. In this situation, redundancy in record keeping (especially when records are maintained by organizationally separate responsible agents) can help establish the accuracy of program participation data.

*Illustration.* The utility of double bookkeeping can be illustrated by the approach used by the Providence school district for keeping track of those students receiving Chapter I instruction. If, for instance, a student in a Chapter I program moves from school x to school y. School x completes a drop form and submits it to the central Chapter I office, indicating that the student is no longer enrolled. As soon as the student arrives, school y sends an add form to the central office, indicating that the student is now enrolled there. If only an add form is received for the student from school y, the central office contacts school x to verify that the student was dropped and requires the form be sent. On the other hand, if an add form has not been received after receiving school x's drop form, school y is contacted to verify that the student has been added and to request that the form be sent. To guard against the effect of neither school submitting the appropriate form, each school's monthly attendance report is compared to the previous month's report. Comparing central office records with school records will reveal any discrepancy in the list of program participants.

## Quality Control

Quality control and the correct implementation of production processes have long been central concerns in industry. Most moderate-sized industrial firms have a department responsible for quality control. Over the past few decades, techniques have been developed to assess and improve quality control in evaluation research.

### *Acceptance Sampling*

*Description.* One quality control strategy that is applicable to evaluation is acceptance sampling. While technical discussions of acceptance sampling techniques can become quite complex (Grant and Leavenworth, 1980), the basic principle is simple to understand. Acceptance sampling begins with the concept of a lot, or group, of data. In a psychiatric treatment setting, for instance, each unit's weekly staff reports on the inpatient clients could be considered lots. In acceptance sampling, every part of every record is not examined. Instead, a sample of each lot is randomly selected and the entire lot is accepted or rejected depending on whether the sample meets predetermined criteria.

*Application.* Crane and Maye (1980) used sampling strategies to assess the frequency of correctable data errors in Chapter I compensatory education evaluation at the State Education Agency (SEA) level. Taking a sample of the results reported to the State of Illinois for several years, they were able to demonstrate that previously undetected errors resulted in a positive bias in the state-aggregated estimate of program effect. Furthermore, their analysis indicated which of several types of errors were most prevalent and deserved the greatest attention in any data correction scheme. Finally, on the basis of their sample, they were able to estimate the average time required to correct each type of error and use these time estimates in planning a cost-efficient data checking strategy.

*Illustration.* An acceptance sampling plan is applicable at several points in the Providence school district evaluation process. For instance, it would be especially valuable when the district evaluation office does its check of test answer sheets before sending them to the correction service. Because this inspection is a time consuming process, there is typically no time to send forms having errors back to the school for correction. The advantage of an acceptance sampling procedure to the district office is evident. In a short time, answer sheets from each school, or even each classroom, could be sampled and the results compared to a predetermined set of criteria. Those lots that failed the test would be returned to the school or classroom level for correction.

This direct, immediate feedback to the school and classroom is lacking in most education evaluations. Typically, because of time constraints and the need to get the tests corrected quickly, classroom teachers do not find out about gross errors until after the evaluation results are already compiled. By then, it is too late to do anything about them. One way to encourage good work would be to make certain that the procedures provide for immediate feedback on performance.

*Cumulative Percentage Charts*

*Description.* The cumulative percentage chart concept derives from what is often termed the Pareto principle described in Juran and Gryna (1970): "Despite the drama of sporadic troubles, the great majority of conformance losses are found to exist in a relatively few chronic troubles. This phenomenon arises from the invariable 'maldistribution' of defects" (p 9–10). To construct a cumulative percentage chart, one needs data on the frequency of some problem or error across a number of units or samples (for instance, hospital wards, prisons, schools). The frequencies are sorted in descending order so that the unit with the greatest amount of error is listed first. These sorted frequencies are converted to percentages of total error and the cumulative percentages are then computed by summing down the percentage column. When these cumulative percentages are plotted, the graph describes the cumulative errors (from most to least) across units.

While a single chart of this type may be useful, the cumulative percentage chart has greater value when multiple problems are graphed together. To accomplish this, one begins by selecting a primary problem area (usually the most serious source of error) and constructing the cumulative percentage chart as described above. For each other problem area of interest, one first constructs the percentage of total error for each unit. Then these percentages are sorted according to the unit order obtained for the primary problem measure. Once sorted, the cumulative percentages are then calculated for each of these additional problem measures. Usually, it is desirable to plot all of these cumulative percentage charts on the same graph so that the relative error contributions of the units on a number of different problems can be assessed simultaneously.

*Application.* These charts, taken together, allow the evaluator to plan for quality control procedures multidimensionally. In a situation where there are resources for general quality control monitoring in only a subset of the relevant units—for instance, in only five jail sites in a state—the evaluator can select the five highest jails on the primary problem measure. The cumulative percentage charts will identify in advance not only what percentage of that problem is likely to be addressed but also what percentage of other relevant quality control problems will be attacked at those five sites. This easily accomplished technique is simple to apply, readily understood, and goes a long way to help target areas that need to improve implementation.

*Illustration.* One of the most serious problems in the Providence evaluation cycle is inaccuracy that occurs when the test answer documents are coded with demographic information and item responses at the school. The extent of the problem becomes clear when the answer documents are received at the evaluation office to be reviewed and packaged for submission to test scoring service. During the most recent test administration, a tabulation was made of the type and frequency of coding errors that occurred in each grade at each school. Figure 4 depicts the actual distribution of coding errors, as represented by a cumulative percentage chart. The dark, solid line depicts the cumulative figures across all grades; the lighter, broken lines provide figures for individual grades. It may be seen that school 1 accounts for about 12 percent of all coding errors, but grade six in school 1 accounts for almost 40 percent of all sixth grade coding errors. The first five schools together were responsible for over 40 percent of all coding problems detected. A quality control program could be effective even if limited in scope to these five schools. It might be even more time and cost-effective if it were concerned only with grades five and six; a program implemented at the other grades would have less to accomplish.

Figure 4. Cumulative Percentage of Total Errors by School for Grades One to Six and Total (Providence Rhode Island School District).

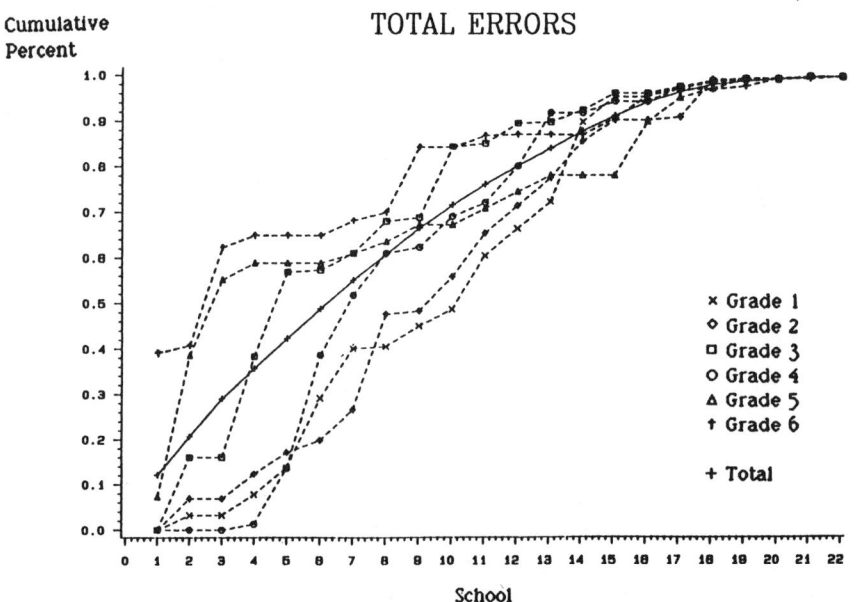

Figure 5. Summary of Selected Quality Control Techniques

| | GENERAL PURPOSE | SPECIFIC PURPOSE | BRIEF DESCRIPTION | SOME ADVANTAGES | SOME DISADVANTAGES |
|---|---|---|---|---|---|
| Internal Control | Prevent Error | Prevent general data errors by ensuring overall system integrity. | Develop a flow-chart description of evaluation system elements, their interrelationships, and key responsible agents. Determine whether the real operation is in compliance with the idea system flowchart. | Also provides for system accountability. A well-described system will improve training efforts. | Can be expensive and time consuming. |
| Double Bookkeeping | Prevent Error | Prevent specific data/information errors. | Develop redundant and/or replicated information recording systems, especially utilizing people who are independent of direct program responsibility. | Specific data errors can be reduced considerably. Enables better auditing of the entire system. | Increases costs. May be hard to defend redundancy in the face of budget constraints. |
| Acceptance Sampling | Identify Error | Identify units having unacceptable error rates. | Conduct random sampling of "lots" of data and inspect each sample for key error indicators. If error in the sample exceeds some predetermined cutoff amount, reject the entire lot. | Cost effective and efficient. | Allows some error to go forward as long as it doesn't exceed some amount/level. |
| Cumulative Percentage Charts | Identify Error | Identify units with the greatest relative error rates. | Calculate percent of error for each unit on one or more variables. Construct cumulative percentage tables and graphs in order to assess the relative contribution | Provides an inexpensive and quick method in targeting quality control efforts so they will have their greatest effect. | Does not allow for weighting of variables in terms of the importance of their errors. |

## Discussion and Conclusion

There are a number of questions that the evaluation methodology community needs to address in order to understand the relative importance that quality control has in conducting a study. This chapter will not attempt to answer such questions, but rather will raise the questions and begin to inform the discussion that is needed.

We can begin by asking how the methods described here are related to each other, and, more generally, how these methods are related to other quality control strategies. Figure 5 summarizes the four methods discussed in terms of their purposes, a brief description of their functioning, and some of the advantages and disadvantages involved in using them. It is clear that the methods differ considerably in their purpose. The strategies that come from the accounting and auditing professions are generally designed to prevent errors from occurring. Internal control procedures do this very generally by trying to ensure that the entire system has integrity and operates sensibly. Double bookkeeping is more targetted to preventing errors on specific variables or forms.

The two approaches that come from industrial quality control are less directed toward preventing error and, instead, are more oriented toward identifying errors that have occurred. If one can identify where errors are happening, it will be easier to construct sensible strategies for preventing the errors from occurring, and so the two notions are not inseparable. Acceptance sampling can be thought of as a weeding out or selection procedure. It often involves identifying those units (schools, prisons, wards, agencies) that fail to meet minimal quality standards. The cumulative percentage chart also uses units but attempts to provide information about the relative contribution to total error that each unit makes.

While each of the methods may be useful in itself, these methods achieve greater effect if they are applied as parts of an integrated quality control program. Internal control procedures could be used to provide the overall structure for the quality control effort because they involve a detailed delineation of the evaluation system. Based on such a flow chart, the evaluator can begin to decide where it is important to have redundancy in information collection procedures (the double bookkeeping notion), where it is necessary or useful to set up quality checks on data lots in order to decide whether to accept the information which units are providing (acceptance sampling), and where it would be useful to study the relative error contributions that units make (cumulative percentage charts) in order to better target quality control resources or training.

The division of methods into those that attempt to prevent error and those that try to identify where it has occurred enables a comparison of these four methods with other approaches. For example, there are a number of analytic traditions in evaluation that involve statistical examination of data for outliers or the effect of attrition. These are similar to acceptance sampling and cumulative percentage charts in that they attempt to identify the location and extent of errors in information. What this suggests is that the rather sketchy taxonomy of quality control methods implied here needs to be extended and critically analyzed if we are to move toward increased quality control.

A central question is how the evaluator decides whether to use quality control methods in an evaluation. Certainly, this issue is directly related to the trade-off between cost and quality. The value of evaluations of different quality is difficult to determine and is likely to remain so. Therefore, questions about gains in quality that might result from the application of quality control techniques are relative. Rather than asking whether an increase in evaluation quality as a result of some procedure balances the costs of the control mechanism, we might ask whether the technique can reduce costs somewhere else in the system. For instance, if an evaluator decides to institute quality criteria checklists that program administrators complete to vouch for the quality of evaluation data collected in their unit, one might look at whether this reduces the need for checks already conducted at a more central organizational office.

Along with testing the relative advantages of alternative control procedures, it is necessary to gain greater experience in applying the strategies in evaluation contexts. To the extent that our strategies require additional workloads, compete with program funds, threaten individuals, or make programs look worse, we can expect resistance from the system. Careful study of attempts to institute quality control programs would help clarify major points of resistance and perhaps suggest alternative approaches.

This chapter has attempted to increase the awareness of evaluators about approaches for assuring evauation data quality that are readily translatable from professions that have had long standing concerns in this area. These approaches are feasible, at least in some contexts as the illustrations presented here indicate. Such approaches, and more, need to be added to the repertoire of techniques that evaluators can apply to improve research quality. It is important that we continue to review the range of quality control options available to us and consider adopting those that could help improve the quality of evaluation research without encountering expense or resistance that could reduce or nullify their impact.

## References

Arens, A. A., and Loebbecke, J. K. *Auditing: An Integrated Approach.* (2nd Ed.) Englewood Cliffs, N.J.: Prentice-Hall, 1980.

Boruch, R. F., and Cordray, D. S. *An Appraisal of Educational Program Evaluations: Federal, State and Local Agencies.* Washington, D.C.: Department of Education, 1980.

Boruch, R. F., Wortman, P. M., and Cordray, D. S., and Associates. *Reanalyzing*

*Program Evaluations: Policies and Practices for Secondary Analysis of Social and Educational Programs.* San Francisco, Calif.: Jossey-Bass, 1981.

Cook, T. D., and Campbell, D. T. *Quasi-Experimentation: Design and Analysis Issues for Field Settings.* Chicago, Ill.: Rand McNally, 1979.

Crane, L. R. *Statistical Quality Control Applications to Chapter I Evaluation Data.* Evanston, Ill.: Educational Testing Service, 1979.

Crane, L. R., and Maye, R. O. "Effects of Correctable Errors on Chapter I NCE Gain Estimates and Implications for Statistical Quality Control." Paper presented at the annual meeting of the American Educational Research Association, Boston, Mass., April 1980.

ERS Standards Committee. "Evaluation Research Society Standards for Program Evaluation." In P. H. Rossi (Ed.), *Standards for Evaluation Practice.* New Directions for Program Evaluation, no. 15. San Francisco, Calif.: Jossey-Bass, 1982.

Glass, G. V., McGaw, B., and Smith, M. L. *Meta-Analysis in Social Research.* Beverly Hills, Calif.: Sage, 1981.

Grant, E. L., and Leavenworth, R. S. *Statistical Quality Control.* New York, N.Y.: McGraw-Hill, 1980.

Hays, W. L. *Statistics for the Social Sciences.* (2nd Ed.) New York, N.Y.: Holt, Rinehart, and Winston, 1973.

Hermanson, R. H., Loeb, S. E., Saada, J. M. and Strawser, R. H. *Auditing Theory and Practice.* Homewood, Ill.: Richard D. Irwin, 1976. Joint Committee on Standards for Educational Evaluation. *Standards for Evaluations of Educational Programs, Projects, and Materials.* New York, N.Y.: McGraw-Hill, 1981.

Juran, J. M., and Gryna, F. M., Jr. *Quality Planning and Analysis.* New York, N.Y.: McGraw-Hill, 1970.

Kish, L. (1965). *Survey Sampling.* New York, N.Y.: Wiley.

Nunnally, J. C. *Psychometric Theory.* New York, N.Y.: McGraw-Hill, 1978. Peragallo, E. *Origin and Evolution of Double Entry Bookkeeping.* New York, N.Y.: American Institute, 1938.

Rosenthal, R. *Meta-Analytic Procedures for Social Research.* Beverly Hills, Calif.: Sage, 1984.

Tabor, J. G. "The Role of the Accountant in Preventing and Detecting Information Abuses in Social Program Evaluation." In T. D. Cook, M. L. DelRosario, K. M. Hennigan, M. M. Mark, and W. M. K. Trochim (Eds.), *Evaluation Studies Review Annual,* (Vol. 3.) Beverly Hills, Calif.: Sage, 1978.

Trochim, W. M. "Research Implementation." Paper presented at the Annual Conference of the Evaluation Research Society, Austin, Tex., October 1981.

Trochim, W. M. *Research Implementation: A Final Report to the National Institute of Education.* Washington, D.C.: National Institute of Education, 1982.

U.S. General Accounting Office *Exposure Draft: The Evaluation Synthesis Method.* Washington, D.C.: U.S. General Accounting Office, 1982.

*William M. K. Trochim is associate professor of human service studies at Cornell University. His research interests include conceptual schemes for evaluation research, selectivity biases in quasi-experimental assessments, and methods for improving the quality of evaluations.*

*Ronald J. Visco is director of evaluation at the Providence, Rhode Island, Public Schools. His research interests include methods for improving evaluations, quality control procedures, and statistical models for assessing achievement.*

# Index

## A

Acceptance sampling: application of, 100; description of, 100; illustration of, 100–101
Accounting, application for quality assurance, 99–100
Aiken, L. R., 9, 26
Ambroz, A., 46
American Psychological Association, 55, 86
Andrews, F., 35, 46
Andrews, W. R., 91
Applied research, 52
Arens, A. A., 94, 105
Attkisson, C. C., 26
Auditing, application for quality assurance, 94–98

## B

Baer, D. M., 53, 59
Baumgartner, R., 35, 46
Bernstein, I. N., 7, 24, 26
Berry, L., 35, 47
Blackburn, B., 46
Boone, C. R., 31, 46
Bootzin, R. R., 37, 45, 46, 58, 60
Boruch, R. F., 2, 5, 9, 10, 26, 30, 32, 47, 80, 89, 90, 93, 105
Bradburn, N. M., 35, 47
Brody, N., 45, 47
Bullook, R. J., 43, 46

## C

Campbell, D. T., 8, 13, 24, 26, 27, 50, 60, 80, 90, 93, 106
Caplan, N., 54, 60
Carver, R. P., 9, 26
Center for Health Services and Policy Research, 30
Chalmers, T. C., 44, 46
Chen, H-T., 2, 5, 10, 27, 64, 73, 77
Cochran, W. G., 35, 46
Coding, 44–45, 82–84, 85, 88–89

Cohen, J., 14, 15, 27, 31, 33, 38, 46, 59, 60, 80, 83, 90, 91
Cohen, P., 80, 91
Combining information, in program planning, 40–41
Confidence rating, 83–84, 85
Cook, T. D., 8, 27, 37–39, 44–46, 50, 60, 63, 67, 71, 77, 78, 93, 106
Cook, T. J., 50, 60
Cordray, D. S., 1–5, 29–48, 58, 60, 76, 82, 86, 87, 90, 91, 93, 105
Coronary Drug Project Research Group, 57, 60
Coulton, C. J., 31, 46
Crane, L. R., 94, 100, 106
Cronbach, L. J., 26, 27, 63, 77
Crosse, S., 1, 7–28
Cumulative percentage charts: application of, 101–102; description of, 101; illustration of, 102
Cunningham, A. E., 41, 47
*Current Index to Journals in Education, The*, 12

## D

Dawes, R., 58, 60
Devine, E. C., 37–39, 44, 46, 71, 77
Division of Personality and Social Psychology, of American Psychological Association, 55
Dole, V. P., 68, 77
Double bookkeeping: application of, 99; description of, 99; illustration of, 99–100
Dunkle, J., 1, 7–28

## E

Effectiveness, treatment, 52
Effects within studies, inclusion of, 43
Efficiency, treatment, 52
Ellett, F. S., 26, 27
Environmental context: as component of program, 64, 66–67; variables of, 66–67

Erlebacher, A. E., 24, 26
Evaluability assessment concept, 10
Evaluation Research Society, Standards Committee of, 94, 106
Experimental paradigm: alternatives to, 26; difficulties inherent in, 8; dominance of, as methodological approach, 12–13; implications of poor methodology in, 25; key aspects of, 8–10; measurement in, 9–10, 16–17; null results in, 10–11; program theory in, 10, 20–23; recommendations for improving, 25–26; research design in, 8–9, 13–14; statistical power in 9–10, 14–16; treatment implementation in, 10, 17–20. *See also* Quantitative synthesis
Eysenck, H. J., 43, 46, 87, 91

**F**

Feeman, D. J., 41, 47
File drawer problem, 43, 80
Finney, J. W., 66, 78
Fisher, K., 85, 91
Fiske, D. W., 87, 91
Flow chart, in internal control, 95–98
Freeman, H. E., 7, 24, 26

**G**

Gibson, F. K., 25, 27
Gilbert, J. P., 44, 47
Glass, G. V., 2, 5, 26, 27, 33, 36, 39, 43, 46, 47, 87, 91–93, 106
Gomez, H., 9, 10, 26, 89, 90
Gordon, G., 7, 12, 24, 27
Grant, E. L., 100, 106
Gryna, F. M., Jr., 101, 106
Guba, E. G., 26, 27

**H**

Hargreaves, W. A., 26
Haring, M. J., 92
Hartmann, D. P., 82, 91
Hays, W. L., 93, 106
Heberlein, T. A., 35, 46
Hedges, L. V., 34, 46, 80, 91
Hendricks, M., 70, 78
Hermanson, R. H., 94, 106
Hirst, E., 35, 47

Hoaglin, D. C., 35, 44, 46
Hogan, R. A., 89, 91
Holland, S., 3, 63–78
Holtzman Report, 93
Horowitz, M. J., 26
Hughes, S. L., 30, 32, 46, 47
Hunter, J. E., 33, 41, 47
Hyde, J. S., 81, 91

**I**

Illinois State Education Agency, education evaluation in, 100
Implementation system: as component of program, 64, 66; variables of, 66
Internal control, 94–98, 104; application of, 95–96; description of, 94–95; illustration of, 96–99
Interrater reliability, 82–83, 85

**J**

Jackson, G. B., 33, 41, 47
Joint Committee on Standards for Educational Evaluation, 94
*Journal of Personality and Social Psychology*, 55
Juran, J. M., 101, 106

**K**

Kazdin, A. E., 51, 60
Keller, S. M., 31, 46
Kenney, D. A., 80, 91
Kerlinger, F. N., 80, 82, 91
Kinney, C., 92
Kirchner, J. H., 89, 91
Kish, L., 93, 106
Knapp, K. M., 89, 91

**L**

Landman, J. T., 58, 60
Leamer, E. E., 34, 47
Leavenworth, R. S., 100, 106
Leviton, L. C., 45, 46
Light, R. J., 2, 5, 16, 24, 27, 33, 34, 45–47, 63, 64, 73, 78, 86, 87, 91
Lincoln, Y. S., 26, 27
Lindeman, C. A., 31, 47
Lipids Research Clinics Program, 53, 60

Lipsey, M. W., 1, 2, 9, 7–28, 30, 36, 50, 60, 65
Loeb, S. E., 106
Loebbecke, J. K., 94, 105
Love, A. J., 67, 78
Lukoff, I. F., 66, 78
Lyall, K. C., 51, 60

**M**

McGaw, B., 2, 5, 33, 44, 46, 47, 91, 106
McPeek, B., 44, 46, 47
Macro-level: judgment calls, 87–89; planning decisions, 29, 76; reporting quality, 80–81
Mark, M. M., 57, 60
Marshall, W. L., 89, 91
Maye, R. O., 94, 100, 106
Measurement: considerations, 41; reliability, 9; sensitivity, 9, 50; of treatment integrity, 54–58; of treatment strength, 54–58; validity, 9
Medicare, 30, 31, 34
Meta-analysis: influence of reporting quality on, 79–86; status of, 43
Methodology, lack of quality in, 7–8, 14–26, 93–94
Michell, W., 30, 47
Micro-level: planning decisions, 29–30, 76; reporting quality, 80–82
Microdata, 86
Miller, T. I., 39, 43, 47, 92
Miller, W., 92
Moos, R. H., 66, 78
Moran, W. C., 82, 91
Morash, M., 74, 78
Morse, E. V., 7, 12, 24, 27
Mosteller, F., 44, 46, 47
Mumford, E., 36, 39–40, 44, 47
Murdock, M., 45, 47

**N**

National Drug and Alcoholism Treatment Utilization Survey, 64, 70–77
National Institute on Drug Abuse, 70–71, 75, 76, 78
Northeastern University, Center for Health Services and Policy Research at, 30
Null results, sources of, 10–11
Nunnally, J. C., 93, 106

Nurius, P. S., 56, 60
Nyswander, M. E., 68, 77

**O**

O'Conner, F., 71, 77
Office of Technology Assessment, 52, 60
Okun, M. A., 92
Olkin, I., 34, 46
Ophuls, W., 85, 91
Orwin, R. G., 3, 4, 30, 35, 36, 39, 43, 44, 46, 47, 79–92

**P**

Pedhazur, E. J., 80, 82, 91
Phillips, M. A., 27, 60, 91
Phillemer, D. B., 2, 5, 33, 34, 45, 47
Pollard, J., 1, 7–28
Poole, W. K., 50, 60
Prather, J. E., 25, 27
Presse, L., 91
Prioleau, L., 45, 47
Program Evaluation Research Group, 11, 12
Program: classification scheme for, theory, 21–22; data base limitations, 76–77; framework for describing, 64–67; impact assessment, 74–75; interactions of, variables, 73–74; research design, 8–10; stability of, measures, 75; theory, 10–11, 20–23; variables, 64–67
Providence (Rhode Island) School District, education evaluation in, 96, 99, 100
*Psychological Abstracts,* 12
Publicizing, quality of, 80–81

**Q**

Qualitative evidence, 45
Quality control, application for quality assurance, 100–103
Quantitative evidence, 45
Quantitative synthesis: confidence rating in, 83–84; deficient reporting in, 84–86; defined, 33; exploiting the by-products of, 34–38; features of, 33–34; implications of, for planning evaluations, 34; importance of sound

Quantitative synthesis *(continued)*
procedures in, 43–44; interrater reliability and, 82–83; judgment calls and, 86–90; major attributes of, 35; reporting quality and, 44, 79–86; status of, 43, steps involved in, 33–34. *See also* Experimental paradigm

## R

Redner, R., 10, 27, 51, 60, 66, 78, 91
Reichardt, C. S., 27
Reitman, D., 46
Reliability, in measurement, 9
Reporting: coding problems in, 44–45; obstacles to improving, 84–85; quality, 44–45, 80–86; sources of, deficiencies, 80–82
Research: aspects of, 8–10; characteristics, 44–45; design, 8–9, 11, 13–14, 24
Riecken, H. W., 30, 32, 47
Rosenthal, R., 34, 43, 47, 80, 91, 93, 106
Rossi, P. H., 2, 5, 10, 27, 29, 47, 51, 60, 64, 73, 77
Rubin, D., 34, 47
Rutman, L., 10, 27

## S

Saada, J. M., 106
St. Pierre, R. G., 67, 71, 78
Sampling, 71
Schlesinger, H. J., 36, 47
Schmidt, F. L., 33, 41, 47
Schroeder, B., 46
Scriven, M., 26, 27
Sechrest, L., 10, 27, 50, 51, 55, 60, 66, 78, 89, 91
Sells, S. B., 67, 78
Shapiro, S. B., 89, 91
Silverman, B., 46
Simpson, D. D., 69, 78
Slavin, R. E., 43, 47
Smith, H., Jr., 46
Smith, M. L., 5, 33, 39, 43, 46, 47, 82–84, 86–89, 91, 92, 106
Smith, P. V., 86, 91
*Sociological Abstracts,* 12
Soderstrom, J., 35, 47
Sonnefeld, L. J., 3, 29–48, 76

Sorensen, J. E., 26
Spiker, V. A., 32, 46
Stanley, J. C., 8, 13, 26
Stanovich, K. E., 41, 47
Statistical power, 9–10, 14–16, 50
Stobart, G., 1, 7–28
Stock, W. A., 82, 92
Stoto, M. A., 46
Strawser, R. H., 106
Studies, inclusion of, 43
Subsystems, in internal control, 94–98
Sudman, S., 35, 47
Svyantek, D. J., 43, 46

## T

Tabor, J. G., 94, 99, 106
Theoretical research, 52
Transaction cycles, in internal control, 94–98
Treatment integrity: and allocation of resources, 59; caveats regarding measures of, 57–58; considerations regarding, 51–54; defined, 51–52; implicit measures of, 53–54; importance of measures of, 50–51; judgment calls and, 89–90; levels of, 52; measuring, 54–58; relation to treatment outcome, 54; relation to treatment strength, 53–54
Treatment strength: and allocation of resources, 59; caveats regarding measures of, 57–58; considerations regarding, 51–54; defined, 51; implicit measures of, 53–54; importance of measures of, 50–51; levels of, 51; measuring, 54–58; relation to treatment integrity, 53–54; relation to treatment outcome, 54
Treatment: as component of program, 64–66; impact of environmental context on, 69; impact of implementation system on, 69; implementation, 10–11, 17–20; as planned versus delivered, 68–69, 71–75; variables of, 65–66. *See also* Treatment integrity, Treatment strength
Trochim, W. M. K., 4, 44, 93–106
Type I errors, 9, 15
Type II errors, 9, 15, 50

## U

U.S. Department of Energy, conservation studies of, 35
U.S. Department of Health and Human Services, 64
U.S. General Accounting Office, 33, 44, 47, 93, 106

## V

Validity, in measurement, 9
Van Aernam, B., 31, 47
Variability, in treatment implementation, 17–20
Visco, R. J., 4, 93–106

## W

Weiss, C. H., 8, 11, 27
Wenk, V., 71, 77
West, S. G., 27, 60, 91
Wholey, J. S., 10, 27
Wolins, L., 2, 5
Wortman, P. M., 2, 5, 24, 27, 56, 60, 90, 93, 105

## Y

Yeaton, W. H., 2, 3, 10, 24, 27, 36, 40, 49–61, 91